RELIGION IN THE HANDMAID'S TALE

RELIGION IN THE HANDMAID'S TALE

A BRIEF GUIDE

Colette Tennant

Fortress Press
Minneapolis

Contents

Introduction

Sometimes a character in a novel will escape its pages and take on a life of her own. Offred from Margaret Atwood's *The Handmaid's Tale* is one such character. She has traveled beyond the bindings of Atwood's novel and is traveling on her own now, not unlike Mary Shelley's Monster or Arthur Conan Doyle's Sherlock Holmes. Offred is a fixture in today's popular culture, so popular that Hulu has promised many more seasons of the show, and Margaret Atwood has written a sequel to the original novel, set fifteen years in the future. Offred is on the move.

Offred knows the Bible well. In fact, she knows it so well that she sometimes catches Aunt Lydia misquoting it. Many of Offred's readers and viewers might not know the Bible as well as she does. This book will help readers and viewers familiarize themselves with the Bible references and echoes saturating both the novel *The Handmaid's Tale* as well as the Hulu series. Recognizing the biblical and religious references that abound in the imaginary dystopia of Gilead, both in the novel's pages and on the television screen, allows readers to understand Gilead in a new way that reveals even more depth and meaning in this powerful story.

By mandate, Offred lives in the newly formed country of Gilead, which calls itself a theocracy. According to the *American Heritage Dictionary*, 3rd edition, a theocracy is "a government ruled by or subject to religious authority." Those in power in Gilead claim divine authority by calling it a theocracy, but readers know that Gilead is actually a dystopia. The *American Heritage Dictionary* defines dystopia as "an imaginary place or state in which the condition of life is extremely bad, as from deprivation, oppression, or terror." The founders of Gilead are men who focus only on the Bible passages (mostly from the Old Testament) that further their agenda: to make themselves as powerful as possible and to subjugate and oppress women.

In a complex way, Atwood uses scriptural references to indict various forms of chauvinism, misogyny, and toxic masculinity, traditions that persistently misread the Bible in defense of their own self-serving stance. At the same time, Atwood uses Scripture to highlight the hypocrisy of the entire Gileadean regime. However, both the novel and the TV series also show characters who are sincere in their faith and use religious names and symbols in significant ways. Understanding these biblical references will help the reader with this kind of multifunctional use of Scripture. The Bible verses quoted in this book, unless otherwise noted, come from the King James Version (KJV) of the Bible as that's the version Gilead quotes or uses most often. Occasionally, a reference comes from the New International Version (NIV), and verses from that translation are identified when they appear.

This book serves as a bridge from the novel and TV series to their biblical references. It focuses on the novel—the foundation of Gilead—but also gives the reader a sense of how the novel's use of religion expands as the Hulu series moves beyond the novel and grows June's story and Gilead's imaginary world. A reader can choose to read this entire book before or after reading *The Handmaid's Tale* and/or watching the Hulu series. Or, thanks to the headings and the index, this book can serve as a reference guide when readers or viewers suspect there is more to be said on a particular subject. We'll move through the religious significance of people and place names, biblical allusions that fill the novel, how religion goes awry as Gilead appropriates and misuses the Bible for its own purposes, the way religion impacts gender and politics in this dystopia, and how the Hulu series depicts Gilead's perverted use of religion. Dive in and understand the world of *The Handmaid's Tale* like never before.

Religious Significance of People and Place Names

It was the language again, I couldn't use it because it wasn't mine. He must have known what he meant but it was an imprecise word; the Eskimos had fifty-two names for snow because it was important to them, there ought to be as many for love.

~ Margaret Atwood, *Surfacing*

People and Titles

Offred

In the introduction to the 2017 Anchor Books edition of *The Handmaid's Tale*, Margaret Atwood comments on the decision to name her main character Offred: "This name is composed of a man's first name, Fred, and a prefix denoting 'belonging to,' so it is like 'de' in French or 'von' in German. . . . Within this name is concealed another possibility: 'offered,' denoting a religious offering or a victim offered for sacrifice" (xv). As Atwood explains in this introductory comment, the name Offred is full of religious significance. In the second part of her comment, Atwood indicates the name denotes "a religious offering." Though the manipulative Aunts attempt to coerce the Handmaids into believing that their new role is heroic, Offred is a victim forced to sacrifice her name, husband, daughter, life, body, and freedom for Gilead's religious society and its desire for children. Each month, she is continually forced to surrender her body in a rape described as a religious ceremony. Significantly, Offred is not associated with biblical women who voluntarily offer themselves and their lives, such as Ruth, who willingly follows her mother-in-law Naomi into a new life, or Esther, who risks death to save the Hebrew people from slaughter. Instead, through her role as a Handmaid, Offred is associated with enslaved women also forced to surrender their bodies and bear children—Bilhah and Zilpah, the biblical handmaids from whom Gilead takes the name and role (more on them later).

Luke

Offred's husband, Luke, shares a name with the author of one of the four Gospels (narratives of the life of Jesus). The Luke of the Bible is the author of the third Gospel as well as the book of Acts. In the novel, we only know Luke through flashbacks. The word *gospel* in English means good news. It makes sense that Luke is named after a Gospel, then, because his character—the memory of his character—is a constant source of love and comfort for Offred. The novel takes care to tell us, though, that Offred's Luke isn't identical to the biblical Luke. The Luke of the Bible is believed to have been a physician (and is referred to as "the beloved physician" in Colossians 4:14); however, Offred tells us that her Luke wasn't a doctor. As she walks past the Wall and sees the dead bodies of executed doctors, Offred feels "relief, because none of these men is Luke. Luke wasn't a doctor. Isn't" (33).

3

Serena Joy

Serena Joy's name reflects two of the gifts of the Holy Spirit listed in Galatians: "But the fruit of the Spirit is love, joy, peace, forbearance, kindness, goodness, faithfulness, gentleness and self-control. Against such things there is no law" (Galatians 5:22–23 NIV). The gifts of the Holy Spirit are considered to be outward attributes of a person with sincere inner beliefs and a model for how people of faith should live. Serena is derived from the word *serene*, which means peaceful or calm. Atwood was being darkly humorous when she chose this name because Serena Joy is anything but peaceful and joyful, and the combination of the two names is incredibly ironic. At their first meeting, when Offred arrives for her new assignment, she looks at Serena Joy's face and sees nothing like a look of joy: "Two lines led downward from the corners of her mouth; between them was her chin, clenched like a fist" (15). Throughout the novel, she is far from peaceful or joyful as she cries during the Ceremony, intentionally causes Offred pain, and seems filled with sorrow and anger at her lack of children and her assigned role in life.

Before the establishment of Gilead, she had been a TV evangelist and a well-known speaker who starred in a television program called the *Growing Souls Gospel Hour*, which suggests an origin for her religiously significant name. Offred ridicules these names that fit her Commander's wife so poorly: "Serena Joy, what a stupid name. It's like something you'd put on your hair, in the other time, the time before, to straighten it. *Serena Joy*, it would say on the bottle, with a woman's head in cut-paper silhouette on a pink oval background with scalloped gold edges" (45). Here the image of the "cut-paper silhouette" suggests Serena Joy's name doesn't have any substance because it doesn't reflect her actual identity.

The Aunts

The Aunts, who train and control the Handmaids, all have names taken from women in the Bible. It's fitting that Gilead would choose to rename female authority figures with biblical names as it continually uses the Bible as a means of asserting its right to the authority and power it has claimed.

Aunt Elizabeth

Aunt Elizabeth shares a name with the biblical Elizabeth, whose story is told in the Gospel of Luke. As the story goes, Elizabeth and her husband, Zechariah, are blessed with a child in their old age. She gives birth to John the Baptist, who will later baptize Jesus. She is pregnant at the same time as her cousin, Mary, the mother of Jesus. Atwood's choice of Elizabeth makes sense in that the biblical character Elizabeth's importance hinges on the significance of pregnancy and childbirth. Also, the biblical Elizabeth gives birth to a child after a long period of infertility, much as Gilead creates the role of Handmaids due to an incredible decline in birthrates and a need for children.

Elizabeth's story is recorded in the first chapter of Luke. According to Luke, when Mary comes to visit her, Elizabeth's baby leaps in her womb. The first words we hear Elizabeth speak are a blessing for the pregnant Mary: "Blessed art thou among women, and blessed is the fruit of thy womb!" (Luke 1:42). This blessing is the source of the traditional greeting the Handmaids give each other when they meet: "Blessed be the fruit." Similarly, these blessings sound like the exhortations Aunt Elizabeth and the other Aunts give to the Handmaids. The Aunts' pep talks to the Handmaids seem like awful parodies of the blessings surrounding Elizabeth and Mary and their miraculous pregnancies and births. Offred recalls these so-called blessings from her time in the training center: "For lunch it was the Beatitudes. Blessed be this, blessed be that. They played it from a tape, so not even an Aunt would be guilty of the sin of reading" (89).

One of Aunt Elizabeth's scenes connected to childbirth occurs during Ofwarren's labor when Aunt Elizabeth plays the role of midwife. She helps bring about the birth of this baby, just as Elizabeth in the Bible announces the forthcoming birth of Mary's child. Ironically, the biblical Elizabeth (and her husband, Zechariah) are called "righteous before God" (Luke 1:6). While the Aunts in *The Handmaid's Tale* claim to have a righteous power that allows them to act as spiritual guides for the Handmaids, they actually abuse and manipulate the women under their control.

AUNT LYDIA

In the book of Acts, Paul, who is called the apostle to the gentiles, baptizes a woman named Lydia on his second missionary journey to what includes modern-day Europe. Lydia is the first person converted to Christianity in Europe. In *The Handmaid's Tale*, considering the enthusiasm the Aunts show for their role, they must have been among the early "converts" in the Republic of Gilead.

The biblical Lydia was a seller of purple cloth, and as such would have interacted with the wealthy and powerful of her day: "One of those listening was a woman from the city of Thyatira named Lydia, a dealer in purple cloth. She was a worshiper of God. The Lord opened her heart to respond to Paul's message. When she and the members of her household were baptized, she invited us to her home. 'If you consider me a believer in the Lord,' she said, 'come and stay at my house.' And she persuaded us" (Acts 16:14–15 NIV). Similarly, Aunt Lydia has worked her way into a powerful position in Gilead. She is one of the most frightening characters in the book as she fervently cheerleads the Handmaids on to their assigned purpose.

Atwood's Aunt Lydia is a parody of the biblical Lydia, a sincere convert to Christianity. Aunt Lydia misquotes the Bible almost any time she tries to reference it. For instance, while she's waiting for Ofglen, Offred remembers one of Aunt Lydia's lessons: "I walk to the corner and wait. I used to be bad at waiting. They also serve who only stand and wait, said Aunt Lydia. She made us memorize it" (18). Aunt Lydia seems to believe this is a biblical maxim she's teaching her Handmaids, but the line actually comes from John Milton's poem "When I Consider How My Light Is Spent."

Aunt Lydia also intentionally misquotes the Bible, trying—and failing—to be humorous. At the beginning of chapter 12, as she bathes, Offred recalls Aunt Lydia's warning about wearing their veil: "Hair must be long but covered. Aunt Lydia said: Saint Paul said it's either that or a close shave. She laughed, that held-back neighing of hers, as if she'd told a joke" (62). Here, Aunt Lydia misquotes a verse from Paul's Letter to the Corinthians: "But every woman who prays or prophesies with her head uncovered dishonors her head—it is the same as having her head shaved" (1 Corinthians 11:5 NIV).

Aunt Lydia misuses Scripture by altering verses to suit her own ends. Offred is astute enough to notice the omission: "You must cultivate poverty of spirit. Blessed are the meek. She [Aunt Lydia] didn't go on to say anything about inheriting the earth" (64). Here, Aunt Lydia has shortened this Beatitude, leaving out any mention of the reward given in the second half. The full Beatitude reads "Blessed are the meek, for they will inherit the earth" (Matthew 5:5 NIV).

AUNT SARA

While Aunt Sara isn't a major character in the novel, her name has a significant biblical connection. In the book of Genesis, Sarah is the wife of the biblical patriarch Abraham. God promises Abraham his descendants will be as numerous as the stars: "I will surely bless you and make your descendants as numerous as the stars in the sky and as the sand on the seashore. Your descendants will take possession of the cities of their enemies" (Genesis 22:17 NIV). Despite this promise, Genesis records that Abraham and Sarah are childless until they are very old. Sarah doubts God will fulfill his promise through her own pregnancy. She sends her handmaid, Hagar, to Abraham to produce a child: "Now Sarai Abram's wife bare him no children: and she had an

9

handmaid, an Egyptian, whose name was Hagar. And Sarai said unto Abram, Behold now, the Lord hath restrained me from bearing: I pray thee, go in unto my maid; it may be that I may obtain children by her. And Abram hearkened to the voice of Sarai" (Genesis 16:1–2). Abraham and Hagar have a son, Ishmael. Sarah, however, eventually becomes pregnant with Isaac, whose son Jacob fathers the twelve tribes of Israel. Jacob's wives, Rachel and Leah, also follow this practice for gaining more children later in the book of Genesis, and the Rachel and Leah Center where the Handmaids are trained in the novel is named for them.

Titles

The Marthas

Every woman in Gilead's housekeeping class has the same title: Martha. Just as the Commander's title becomes his name, so the housekeepers have a title as their name. The designers of Gilead's society picked a fitting name for this group of women since the character Martha in the New Testament (described in the Gospels of Luke and John) is especially known for fretting over housework.

In the Bible, Jesus visits Martha, her sister Mary, and their brother Lazarus. Mary sits at Jesus's feet and listens to every word he says while Martha complains about her sister not helping her do housework:

> As Jesus and his disciples were on their way, he came to a village where a woman named Martha opened her home to him. She had a sister called Mary, who sat at the Lord's feet listening to what he said. But Martha was distracted by all the preparations that had to be made. She came to him and asked, "Lord, don't you care that my sister has left me to do the work by myself? Tell her to help me!" "Martha, Martha," the Lord answered, "you are worried and upset about many things, but few things are needed—or indeed only one. Mary has chosen what is better, and it will not be taken away from her." (Luke 10:38–42 NIV)

The Gilead regime uses one woman's story as a way to identify the prescribed role for this entire class.

Sons of Jacob

The founders of Gilead call themselves Sons of Jacob. This phrase might sound innocuous enough, but for those who have read their story in Genesis, it's a chilling appropriation. In Genesis, God promises Abraham, and then

11

Abraham's son Isaac and Isaac's son Jacob, that they will be blessed with countless offspring. God promises Jacob "Your descendants will be like the dust of the earth, and you will spread out to the west and to the east, to the north and to the south. All peoples on earth will be blessed through your offspring" (Genesis 28:10–14 NIV). Jacob has twelve sons, who found the twelve tribes of Israel, God's chosen people. When the men who founded Gilead take on this name, they are trying to claim a direct blessing from God—that they are God-ordained patriarchs destined to rule.

Handmaids

As Sons of Jacob, the founders of Gilead assert that they are entitled to Handmaids in order to produce children if their wives cannot or can no longer have children. Handmaids are fertile women young enough to bear children. These women have been wrenched from their former lives and forced into compliance by the Aunts at the Rachel and Leah Center. The concept of a handmaid goes all the way back to the earliest stories in the Bible. The first words Atwood includes in the novel are an epigraph from Genesis, when Rachel offers up her handmaid to her husband Jacob:

And when Rachel saw that she bare Jacob no children, Rachel envied her sister; and said unto Jacob,
Give me children, or else I die. And Jacob's anger
was kindled against Rachel: and he said, Am I in
God's stead, who hath withheld from thee the fruit
of the womb? And she said, Behold my maid Bilhah, go in unto her; and she shall bear upon my
knees, that I may also have children by her. (Genesis 30:1–3)

A few chapters before the story of Jacob, Rachel, and
Bilhah, we find the story of Sarah and Abraham and Sarah's handmaid Hagar, which is the first recorded use of a
handmaid in Genesis. In the story quoted in the epigraph
to *The Handmaid's Tale*, Jacob's wives compete with each
other over fertility. In Genesis, Jacob leaves his parents,
Isaac and Rebekah, and returns to the land of his mother's
family. When he does, he meets Rachel and agrees to work
for her father, Laban, for seven years in exchange for marrying Rachel. After the seven years pass, Laban tricks Jacob
into marrying his older daughter, Leah, first and Jacob
then works seven more years to marry the woman he truly
wants: Rachel. Leah, Jacob's least favorite wife, is very fertile and produces many children. His favorite wife, Rachel,
struggles to become pregnant and becomes desperate to

have children of her own. Leah, not to be outdone by her sister, also wants more children. Rachel and Leah both send their handmaids to Jacob in order to gain more children through them.

Offred repeats one of the verses from the epigraph when she visits the doctor, and he offers to "help" her get pregnant. "*Give me children, or else I die.* There's more than one meaning to it" (61). The repetition of this phrase offers a second glance at the biblical foundations of Offred's role. Before the Ceremony, the Commander reads passages from the Bible to his household, including "the moldy old Rachel and Leah stuff we had drummed into us at the Center. *Give me children, or else I die. Am I in God's stead, who hath withheld from thee the fruit of the womb / Behold my maid Bilhah. She shall bear upon my knees, that I may also have children by her*" (88). Gilead interprets this passage literally, and the Ceremony for Commanders, Handmaids, and Wives involves the Handmaids being literally placed on, or between, the Wife's knees during sex (the rape of the Handmaids) and birth. The founders of Gilead reinstitute this Old Testament practice and develop a whole class of Handmaids they use as they see fit, claiming them as a God-given right.

14

The Eyes

The Eyes are everywhere in Gilead, watching Handmaids in particular, to make sure they follow their prescribed roles. Early on, Offred suspects Nick of being an Eye. The founders of Gilead, in creating this group of watchers, borrow the idea of God's all-seeing nature. Thus, they are implying that what their Eyes see is what God sees, conflating their intent with God's. Before the Ceremony, the Commander reads a Bible verse describing the Eyes: "For the eyes of the Lord run to and fro throughout the whole earth, to shew himself strong in the behalf of them whose heart is perfect toward him" (2 Chronicles 16:9). In Gilead's dystopia, this verse gives the Eyes power to arrest, torture, and kill anyone suspected of not being an ideal member of Gileadean society.

Commanders of the Faithful and Guardians of the Faith

Just as women in Gilead are given religiously based titles and roles, so are the men. Powerful men with leadership roles in Gilead are given the full title "Commander of the Faithful," while men who work for them, like Nick, are called "Guardian of the Faith." Both titles give men authority based on their roles as those who care for, or protect, the rest of Gilead (referred to as "the faithful").

Angels

Angels appear in the Bible, typically as bearers of good news or as protectors. Gilead chooses to call its soldiers *Angels* as a way to assert the divine authority of their armies and condone the violence they enact.

Behemoths, Whirlwinds, and Chariots

The founders of Gilead are so thorough in establishing their theocracy that even car models have names from the Bible. Offred tells us that cars are either Behemoths, Whirlwinds, or Chariots. *Behemoth* refers to some kind of large animal and appears in the book of Job as God describes his creation: "Behold now behemoth, which I made with thee; he eateth grass as an ox. Lo now, his strength is in his loins, and his force is in the navel of his belly" (Job 40:15–16). Earlier in Job, God "answered Job out of the whirlwind" (Job 38:1). Whirlwinds appear in several other places in the Bible as a sign of God's power; for example, Jeremiah 23:19 describes "a whirlwind of the Lord is gone forth in fury." Chariots appear in the

Bible as a method of transportation, especially in war or as a sign of power and wealth.

Places

Gilead

Gilead, the land of Atwood's dystopia, appears in several places in the Bible. The first, and most relevant reference, is in Genesis. Jacob, the grandson of Abraham and favored son of Isaac, lives with Rachel, Leah, their handmaids, and his children under the rule of his father-in-law, Laban, for twenty years. Eventually, Jacob decides to take his family and property and return to his own country. Basically, Jacob sneaks away with his wives and children and sets "his face toward the mount Gilead" (Genesis 31:21). He pitches his tents in Gilead, this new land, which is later part of the area where the tribes of Israel live. The founders of Atwood's Gilead claim the name *Gilead* as the name of the land of the Sons of Jacob.

While the Sons of Jacob take on the name Gilead as a sign of their destined rule, the biblical allusion is more complicated. When Laban finds Jacob in Gilead, he laments, "These daughters are my daughters, and these children are my children" (Genesis 31:43), making Gilead the land of the stolen daughters. Jacob's search for a place where he can own outright his wives and handmaids, and be the primary authority figure, begins in Gilead. Likewise, Atwood's Republic of Gilead is the land of many stolen daughters—Offred and her daughter, every Handmaid there, even every Wife bereft of her former freedom, all of them owned by a man in some way. In the lesser-known book of Hosea, there is a haunting description of Gilead, which sounds stunningly like Atwood's Republic of Gilead: "Gilead is a city of evildoers, stained with footprints of blood" (Hosea 6:8 NIV). The Republic of Gilead, with its Wall and Particicutions, is definitely stained with footprints of blood. The Handmaids are dressed in the color of blood. Early in the novel, Offred catches sight of herself in a mirror and describes herself as "a Sister, dipped in blood" (9), and just before that she describes her proscribed uniform: "Everything except the wings around my face is red: the color of blood, which defines us" (8). The idea of blood here speaks both to the threat of physical violence the Handmaids endure as well as their female sexuality, which is completely co-opted.

The book of Amos also refers to Gilead: "This is what the Lord says: 'For three sins of Ammon, even for four, I will not relent. Because he ripped open the pregnant women of Gilead in order to extend his borders'" (Amos 1:13 NIV). In

Atwood's Gilead, the powerful Commanders of Gilead have raped the fertile women in order to expand their population and maintain the power and growth of their own nation.

At the beginning of the Prayvaganza, the assembled women sing a spiritual entitled "There Is a Balm in Gilead." The phrase "balm in Gilead" comes from the book of Jeremiah, where the prophet cries: "Since my people are crushed, I am crushed; I mourn, and horror grips me. Is there no balm in Gilead? Is there no physician there? Why then is there no healing for the wound of my people?" (Jeremiah 8:21–22 NIV). The lyrics for the spiritual are more hopeful than the Scripture verse, though Offred doesn't tell us if the Republic of Gilead changes the lyrics:

> There Is a Balm in Gilead
> Sometimes I feel discouraged and think my work's in vain,
> But then the Holy Spirit revives my soul again.
> There is a balm in Gilead to make the wounded whole;
> There is a balm in Gilead to heal the sin sick soul.
> If you cannot preach like Peter, if you cannot pray like Paul,
> You can tell the love of Jesus and say, "He died for all."

There is a balm in Gilead to make the wounded
    whole;

There is a balm in Gilead to heal the sin sick soul.

Don't ever feel discouraged, for Jesus is your friend;

And if you lack for knowledge, He'll never refuse
    to lend.

There is a balm in Gilead to make the wounded
    whole;

There is a balm in Gilead to heal the sin sick soul.

Rachel and Leah Center (The Red Center)

The name of the Rachel and Leah Center comes from Genesis and its story of Rachel and Leah, the wives of Jacob. As the Handmaid training center, the Bilhah and Zilpah Center would have been more congruent with the respective character roles in the Bible. However, by naming the center for Rachel and Leah, the founders of Gilead at once obscure the personhood of the biblical handmaids while highlighting the women responsible for appropriating the bodies of their subordinates. By naming the Center after the wives of the biblical patriarch, Jacob, they are, again, claiming their patriarchal right to such a system.

All Flesh

Every store or business mentioned in the Republic of Gilead takes its name from the Bible. In this way, the founders of the society emphasize their supposed piety and assert the authority of their theocracy. All Flesh comes from Genesis 6:13, as God speaks to Noah about the coming flood: "And God said unto Noah, The end of all flesh is come before me; for the earth is filled with violence through them; and, behold, I will destroy them with the earth." The phrase appears in other places throughout the Bible, as well. For example, Isaiah 40:6 reads "The voice said, Cry. And he said, What shall I cry? All flesh is grass, and all the goodliness thereof is as the flower of the field." And 1 Peter 1:24 says "For all flesh is as grass, and all the glory of man as the flower of grass. The grass withereth, and the flower thereof falleth away." The context in which the phrase is used in the Bible is usually one of death, making this a fitting name for a butcher shop.

Lilies of the Field

Offred describes Lilies of the Field: "The store has a huge wooden sign outside it, in the shape of a golden lily. . . .

You can see the place, under the lily, where the lettering was painted out, when they decided that even the names of shops were too much temptation for us. Now places are known by their signs alone" (25). Offred remembers the store used to be a movie theater where men and women went "on their own, making up their minds" (25). Lilies of the Field is the store where Handmaids order uniforms. The name comes from a verse in the book of Luke: "Consider the lilies how they grow: they toil not, they spin not; and yet I say unto you, that Solomon in all his glory was not arrayed like one of these" (Luke 12:27). In the Bible, this verse is a reassurance of God's providence; however, in Gilead it's used manipulatively. By calling the store that sells the prescribed Handmaids uniform "Lilies of the Field," the orchestrators of Gilead's society suggest that the Handmaids are "arrayed" or dressed in a glorious or fitting and appropriate way for their role, and that their role is a providential one instead of a prison.

Milk and Honey

The men who run Gilead, by using names for stores like *Milk and Honey* and *Lilies of the Field*, work to convince the citizens there that they are well taken care of. The lilies verse in Luke references God's care for his people, but in Gilead, it is the rulers who fill the role of God and insure the well-being of its citizens. Similarly, Milk and Honey, Offred and Ofglen's first stop on their initial shopping trip together, references a promise of divine reward and abundance. The name Milk and Honey comes from God's promise to the Israelites regarding what awaits them in the promised land. Leviticus 20:24 NIV says: "But I said to you, 'You will possess their land; I will give it to you as an inheritance, a land flowing with milk and honey. I am the Lord your God, who has set you apart from the nations.'" This verse, with its language of possession, promise, and abundance, aligns with the leaders' claim that they are the Sons of Jacob and divinely ordained to their roles and power. It also suggests to the citizens of Gilead that they have an abundance, that their needs for food are met. Further, it connects possession and flowing milk, which summarizes what Gilead expects of its Handmaids. The men who run Gilead claim the country and the women in it as their possessions and set the women apart for a particular type of abundance: to offer up their offspring to fulfill what the republic's propaganda promises to be a larger purpose.

Loaves and Fishes

The name of this store comes from one of Jesus's most famous miracles. A huge crowd follows Jesus and the disciples, and

23

they have nothing to eat. A little boy gives Jesus a basket of bread and fish. Jesus takes it, miraculously multiplies it, and feeds the five thousand men present, as well as the women and children who are with them. This store's name is a misnomer on many counts. They don't even sell bread there, and they rarely sell fish because the environment has deteriorated so much fish are hardly ever available. Gilead again appropriates a phrase from the Bible to create its own version of reality. There is nothing particularly satisfying, let alone miraculous, about this store. Offred tells us, "Loaves and Fishes is hardly ever open" (164).

Daily Bread

In the book of Matthew, Jesus's disciples ask him how to pray, and in reply, he prays what is commonly called "The Lord's Prayer." The name of this store comes from the phrase within that prayer, "Give us this day our daily bread," (Matthew 6:11). Much like Loaves and Fishes, the name here is meant to indicate Gilead's ability to meet its citizens' needs; however, it actually functions as an ironic reminder of the lack of resources in Gilead. Jesus uses the phrase to make the point that his disciples need God's spiritual food daily. Atwood portrays the exact opposite in Gilead's twisted imitation of a godly kingdom: "It [Loaves and Fishes] doesn't

24

sell loaves though. Most households bake their own, though you can get dried-up rolls and wizened doughnuts at Daily Bread, if you run short" (164). This misnamed store hardly offers its shoppers daily sustenance of any kind.

Soul Scrolls

This store name combines two familiar religious words that together sound pious, although the actual phrase doesn't appear in the Bible. Ancient versions of the Bible are written on scrolls, most famously the Dead Sea Scrolls. Soul Scrolls is a place where citizens of Gilead can go to order automatic prayers.

Jezebel's

The word *Jezebel* is an eponym in our culture; it refers to a woman who is considered loose or evil in some way. Jezebel's story comes from 1 Kings. She is a Phoenician princess who marries Ahab, the king of the Northern Kingdom of Israel. She insists that this kingdom worship Baal instead of Yahweh (God), whose prophets she kills. When Ahab loses power and Jehu takes control, Jezebel dies a horrible death. The Bible describes Jezebel putting on makeup before her death: "And when Jehu was come to Jezreel, Jezebel heard of it; and she painted her face, and [at]tired her head, and looked out at a window" (2 Kings 9:30). Jehu orders that Jezebel be thrown out of the window, and her body is eaten by dogs. Because of the biblical story, Jezebel's name has been associated with sexuality, with evil, and with a woman damned for her sins. In *The Handmaid's Tale*, Jezebel's is the nickname given to nightclub/brothel the Commanders have devised for their own pleasures where women like Moira who would not conform are sent.

2

Biblical Allusions

I'm a strict, strict agnostic. It's very different from a casual, "I don't know." It's that you cannot present as knowledge something that is not knowledge. You can present it as faith, you can present it as belief, but you can't present it as fact.

~ Margaret Atwood, Interview
with *Narrative* Magazine

Phrases

Blessed Be the Fruit

Ofglen's first spoken words in the novel are "Blessed be the fruit" when she meets Offred for the first time (19). This phrase is a shortened Bible verse that reads more fully, "Blessed is the fruit of thy womb" (Luke 1:42). The most well-known use of this phrase in the Bible comes from a scene early in Luke's story of Jesus's birth. Mary, who is pregnant with Jesus, goes to see her cousin Elizabeth, who is also pregnant with her own child. When Elizabeth sees Mary, her baby moves in her womb, and she exclaims to Mary: "Blessed art thou among women, and blessed is the fruit of thy womb" (Luke 1:42). The founders of Gilead shorten the verse to refer not to the woman but to what her body can produce: children. By having Handmaids greet each other with these words, Gilead reminds the Handmaids repeatedly that their sole purpose and value in this society is their ability to give birth to a healthy child.

May the Lord Open

When Ofglen greets Offred with "Blessed be the fruit," Offred replies, "May the Lord open," which she notes to the reader

is "the accepted response" (19). In Rachel and Leah's story in
the Bible, verses frequently refer to their wombs being closed
or opened by God. Genesis 29:31 says, "And when the Lord
saw that Leah was hated, he opened her womb: but Rachel
was barren." The phrase also describes Rachel, Leah's sister and Jacob's favored wife: "And God remembered Rachel,
and God hearkened to her, and opened her womb" (Genesis
30:22). The phrase fits the roles the Handmaids are forced
into and shows how even the smallest details of Rachel and
Leah's story are used to constrain and control the Handmaids
and their bodies.

Praise Be

Also in the first scene with Ofglen and Offred, Offred repeats
another stock phrase three times: "Praise be" (19–20). Like
"Blessed be the fruit," this phrase is shortened, kind of dangling, because the reader is left to question, Praise be what
or whom? Christians would complete the phrase "Praise be
to God" or "Praise God," but in Gilead, it's just "Praise be."
Many of the psalms contain the phrase "Praise be": "Praise
be to the Lord, the God of Israel, from everlasting to everlasting. Amen and Amen" (Psalm 41:13 NIV); "Praise be to
the Lord from Zion, to him who dwells in Jerusalem. Praise
the Lord" (Psalm 135:21 NIV); and "Praise be to God, who

has not rejected my prayer or withheld his love from me!" (Psalm 66:20 NIV). The biblical phrase always directs its praise toward God, but not so in Gilead. God is not really mentioned that often by those living in this dystopia. The omission of God from this phrase hints that religion is used as a means of control and authority, but that Gilead is not led by people filled with genuine faith.

Under His Eye

Much as "Blessed be the fruit" and "May the Lord open" are the acceptable greetings between Handmaids, there is also an acceptable farewell: "under his eye" (45). The presence of the Eyes and the sense of being watched occur frequently in the novel. Most obviously, the secret government spies who exert significant power in Gilead and work to maintain the theocracy's total control are called the Eyes. When Offred remembers how she and Luke had to kill their cat when they were trying to escape, she repeats the Gilead propaganda: "The Eyes of God run over all the earth" (193). This is a fairly direct quote from 2 Chronicles: "For the eyes of the Lord run to and fro throughout the whole earth, to shew himself strong in the behalf of them whose heart is perfect toward him" (2 Chronicles 16:9). Those in power in Gilead keep their control by constantly watching every member of the society to be sure they are fulfilling their prescribed roles. The repeated phrase "under his eye" emphasizes the total authority of Gilead's government and the extent to which its citizens are watched.

Eyes also appear as a symbol. Offred's tattoo contains the eye symbol: "I cannot avoid seeing, now, the small tattoo on my ankle. Four digits and an eye, a passport in reverse" (65). The eye here emphasizes the sight and control of the government. Offred continues with the description, "It's supposed to guarantee that I will never be able to fade, finally, into another landscape. I am too important, too scarce, for that. I am a national resource" (65). She and the other Handmaids are things, objectified, controlled, and constantly watched.

Symbols

Communion

Communion in the Catholic and Protestant churches alike is often the centerpiece of a worship service, where believers eat bread and drink wine as an act of remembering Christ's sacrifice on the cross. Christ instituted the act of Communion at the Last Supper with his disciples the night before he was crucified, and a version of this first Communion appears in the books of Matthew, Mark, Luke, and John in the Bible. In the Protestant church, Communion is practiced as a symbolic act while the Catholic Church believes in transubstantiation: that the wine and bread actually become the blood and body of Christ. The elements or ideas of Communion appear symbolically in the novel. For example, when the Commander sneaks Offred into his office, Offred thinks, "To him, I'm not just a boat with no cargo, a chalice with no wine in it, an oven—to be crude—minus the bun. To him I am not merely empty" (163). Here we see Atwood explicitly refer to the elements of Communion: chalice (which holds the wine), wine, bun (bread).

Similarly, when the Handmaids gather to witness Janine give birth, they experience a brief hint of Communion. They are allowed to drink spiked grape juice, and Offred says, "We grip each other's hands, we are no longer single" (125). Much later in the novel, Atwood gives us a similar impression of Communion when Serena Joy allows Offred to glimpse a photograph of her daughter. This heartbreaking scene describes the brief moment Offred sees what her daughter looks like now: "My treasure. So tall and changed. Smiling a little now, so soon, and in her white dress as if for an olden-days First Communion" (228).

Lilies

Lilies appear in many places in *The Handmaid's Tale*. The store for clothes is called Lilies of the Field, Serena Joy wears perfume called Lily of the Valley, and Offred's room has a pillow with the word *faith* and "a wreath of lilies" embroidered on it (57). While the Lilies of the Field name comes from a verse in Luke, Serena Joy's perfume alludes to the Song of Songs: "I am a rose of Sharon, a lily of the valley" (Song of Songs 2:1 NIV). In this verse, Solomon's lover is claiming she is a rose, a lily. Solomon affirms this metaphor in the following verse, "Like a lily among thorns is my darling among young women" (Song of Songs 2:2 NIV). In a Christian context, "Lily of the Valley" also refers to a hymn that describes Christ as "the lily of the valley."

Symbolically, lilies are frequently associated with Mary, the mother of Jesus. Depictions of the annunciation (the angel Gabriel coming to Mary to tell her she will give birth to the son of God) frequently include lilies, intended to symbolize Mary's purity as a virgin. Significantly, the color blue, which is worn by the Wives in Gilead, is also frequently associated with the Virgin Mary. Her association with blue comes from a couple of places. First, in the Old Testament, the ark of the covenant is covered in "a cloth wholly of blue"

(Numbers 4:6). Mary, who carries Christ, the sign of the new covenant, is thus associated with blue as well. Also, blue is considered the color of the sky or the heavens and, therefore, is appropriate for the mother of Christ.

Serena Joy's Garden

When Offred first arrives at the Commander's house, she leaves her room occasionally, and one place she goes is to the garden, which is Serena Joy's territory. Offred comments more than once about Serena Joy's garden. The first time she describes it, she notices "a willow, weeping catkins . . . daffodils are now fading and the tulips are opening their cups, spilling out color" (12). Every scene in the garden is ironic because it's Serena Joy's garden, a sign of fertility and growth, but she is infertile and unable to have a child. Serena Joy's garden is a reverse Eden: in the garden of Eden in the book of Genesis, God commands Adam and Eve to be fruitful and multiply, but Serena Joy cannot be fruitful and multiply. Infertility symbols pile up here: weeping catkins, fading daffodils. Even during the Ceremony, Serena Joy literally wreathes herself in flowers. Offred describes what she sees: "She's in one of her best dresses, sky blue with embroidery in white along the edges of the veil: flowers and fretwork. Even at her age she still feels the urge to wreathe herself in flowers. No use for you, I think at her, my face unmoving, you can't use them anymore, you're withered. They're the genital organs of plants" (81–82). A more apt view of Serena Joy's relationship to flowers occurs when Offred watches her in her garden: "She was snipping off the seedpods with a pair of sheers" (153). Offred witnesses her aggression and wonders, "some blitzkrieg, some kamikaze, committed on the swelling genitalia of the flowers?" (153). Serena Joy, unable to have children, ironically appears surrounded by flowers in her reverse Eden but also takes out her anger and frustration on the fertile plants.

The Lamb

Lambs, a symbol of religious sacrifice, appear throughout the novel. In the Bible, Jesus is greeted with "Behold the Lamb of God, which taketh away the sin of the world," a reference to his sacrificial death on the cross for the redemption of humankind (John 1:29). When the Commander's household gathers in the sitting room before the Ceremony, Offred notices on the mantel "a white china Cupid . . . its arms around the neck of a lamb" (80). Earlier in the novel, when she's shopping with Ofglen, Offred's observations about the clouds in the sky echo the idea of a sacrificial lamb: "We walk, sedately. The sun is out, in the sky there are white fluffy clouds, the kind that look like headless sheep" (30). The sacrificial-lamb image connects with Atwood's description of Offred's name as relating to being offered up, especially in the sense of a sacrifice.

Biblical Quotations

Gilead's authority figures frequently use Bible verses, or passages that supposedly come from the Bible, as justification for their laws, society, and abuses. Sometimes they use verses that actually appear in the Bible, sometimes they take verses from multiple places in the Bible and present them as if they appear together in a single passage, and sometimes they omit key phrases from verses or make verses up. In all these instances, Gilead twists and manipulates the Bible to serve its own ends rather than attempting to genuinely understand and follow the Bible's teachings.

The Beatitudes

During lunch at the Rachel and Leah Center, the Handmaids listen to a tape of what are supposedly the Beatitudes. The Beatitudes are a set of blessings that Jesus speaks during his famous Sermon on the Mount in the book of Matthew. The Beatitudes the Handmaids listen to say "Blessed be the poor in spirit, for theirs is the kingdom of heaven. Blessed are the merciful. Blessed be the meek. Blessed are the silent.... Blessed be those that mourn, for they shall be comforted" (89). Offred is astute and biblically literate enough to realize "they made that up, I knew it was wrong, and they left things out, too" when she hears "blessed are the silent." The actual Beatitudes in Matthew read:

> Blessed are the poor in spirit, for theirs is the kingdom of heaven. Blessed are those who mourn, for they will be comforted. Blessed are the meek, for they will inherit the earth. Blessed are those who hunger and thirst for righteousness, for they will be filled. Blessed are the merciful, for they will be shown mercy. Blessed are the pure in heart, for they will see God. Blessed are the peacemakers, for they will be called children of God. Blessed are those who are persecuted because of righteousness, for theirs is the kingdom of heaven. (Matthew 5:3–10 NIV)

Gilead adds in "silent," a value of its own not spoken by Jesus, and leaves out the meek's inheritance of the earth and the act of being shown mercy, as well as the call to peace, as these do not match its violent ends and desire to remain in power.

The Penalty for Rape

Before the Particicution, the ceremony during which Handmaids execute men accused of crimes like rape, Aunt Lydia reminds the Handmaids that death is the penalty for rape and cites (but does not read or recite) Deuteronomy 22:23–29, a passage that describes Old Testament laws about sexual assault, including death as the punishment for a man who rapes a woman engaged to be married.

The Ceremony

Before the Ceremony, the household gathers in the living room for the Commander to read the Bible. The passages chosen for the pre-Ceremony ritual are carefully selected by Gilead to justify the Ceremony. The Commander reads God's command to Adam and Eve in the garden of Eden, "Be fruitful, and multiply, and replenish the earth" (Genesis 1:28), repeated to Noah in Genesis 9:1 after the biblical flood that destroyed the earth. He also reads the passages from Genesis describing Rachel, Leah, and their handmaids Bilhah and Zilpah. Gilead selects passages that suit its ends—needing women to give birth to healthy children—and uses them to frame and justify rape.

In the midst of the Ceremony, as Serena Joy digs her rings into Offred's hands, Offred remembers, "This is supposed to signify that we are one flesh" (94). Here, Offred recalls a verse from Ephesians, "For this reason a man will leave his father and mother and be united to his wife, and the two will become one flesh" (Ephesians 5:31 NIV). The key word in Offred's recollection is *supposed* as she recognizes there aren't two united to become one flesh here; there are three. It is an act of rape, not marriage.

The Ceremony itself, with the posture of the Handmaid between the wife's legs, comes from an extremely literal interpretation of the biblical passages describing Rachel, Leah, and their handmaids Bilhah and Zilpah. In Genesis 30, Rachel tells Jacob "Behold my maid Bilhah, go in unto her; and *she shall bear upon my knees*, that I may also have children by her" (Genesis 30:3).

Marriage

Gilead's wedding ceremony relies heavily on biblical justification for men oppressing and subjugating women. The Commander performing the ceremony reads, "I will that women adorn themselves in modest apparel . . . with shamefacedness and sobriety; not with braided hair, or

39

gold, or pearls, or costly array"; "Let the woman learn in silence with *all* subjection"; "But I suffer not a woman to teach, not to usurp authority of the man, but to be in silence." "For Adam was first formed, then Eve. And Adam was not deceived, but the woman being deceived was in the transgression. Notwithstanding she shall be saved by child-bearing, if they continue in faith and charity and holiness with sobriety" (221). These elements from the marriage ceremony, used to justify the treatment of women, come from 1 Timothy. In this book, Paul talks about how women should dress and behave during worship:

> In like manner also, that women adorn themselves in modest apparel, with shamefacedness and sobriety; not with braided hair, or gold, or pearls, or costly array; But (which becometh women professing godliness) with good works. Let the woman learn in silence with all subjection. But I suffer not a woman to teach, nor to usurp authority over the man, but to be in silence. For Adam was first formed, then Eve. And Adam was not deceived, but the woman being deceived was in the transgression. Notwithstanding she shall be saved in child-bearing, if they continue in faith and charity and holiness with sobriety (1 Timothy 2:9–15).

These verses are very useful to the men who established Gilead. They not only supposedly demonstrate how women are to be patronized because they are not to be trusted since, like Eve, they could be easily deceived, but also the verses justify viewing women as mainly useful for childbearing. By including these verses in a marriage ceremony, the Commanders ignore that Paul here specifically refers to women's roles in worship, not in marriage. They would also have had to ignore other passages where Paul stressed the fact that it was Adam's sin that brought death into the world—such as Romans 5:14 NIV: "Nevertheless, death reigned from the time of Adam to the time of Moses, even over those who did not sin by breaking a command, as did Adam, who is a pattern of the one to come"—as well as Paul's role as one of the authors of the Bible, a book that includes many strong women who play vital roles in its narrative. Rather than understanding the verses in context, Gilead appropriates verses that speak to the values it imposes on others.

Biblical Concepts

The Lord's Prayer

Offred prays or reflects on the act of prayer at several points in the novel. In chapter 30, in a heart-wrenching scene, she tries to recite a version of the Lord's Prayer. The Lord's Prayer refers to a prayer Christ speaks in the book of Matthew when his disciples ask him how they should pray. It is the biblical model for prayer. The biblical version goes as follows:

> After this manner therefore pray ye: Our Father which art in heaven, Hallowed be thy name.
> Thy kingdom come, Thy will be done in earth, as it is in heaven.
> Give us this day our daily bread.
> And forgive us our debts, as we forgive our debtors.
> And lead us not into temptation, but deliver us from evil: For thine is the kingdom, and the power, and the glory, for ever. Amen. (Matthew 6:9–13)

Offred tries praying a version of this sitting in the window seat by her FAITH pillow:

> My God. Who Art in the Kingdom of Heaven, which is within.
> I wish you could tell me Your Name, the real one I mean. But *You* will do as well as anything.
> I wish I knew what You were up to. But whatever it is, help me to get through it, please. . . .
> I have enough daily bread, so I won't waste time on that. It isn't the main problem. . . .

> Now we come to forgiveness. Don't worry about for-
> giving me . . . keep the others safe, if they are
> safe. Don't let them suffer too much. . . . You
> might even provide a Heaven for them. . . .
> Deliver us from evil.
> Then there's Kingdom, power, and glory. It takes
> a lot to believe in those right now. But I'll try it
> anyway. (194–95)

Offred's version of the prayer reveals a desire for faith and hope as well as a struggle to believe in or know God in her horrifying circumstances. She ends with "Oh God. It's no joke. Oh God oh God. How can I keep on living?" (195).

Messiah Figure

In the Bible, Jesus fulfills the role of the Messiah figure, especially in his sacrificial death. Certain echoes in the novel connect Offred to the concept of a messiah figure. Her name itself, as discussed in chapter 1, labels her as a kind of sacrifice. In the novel, Offred tells us "I am thirty-three years old" (143), which is the same age many consider Jesus to have been at the time of his death. Other images invit-ing a comparison of Offred to a messiah figure accumulate when Offred finds the hidden message "*nolite te bastardes carborundorum*." Offred tells us she discovers the message three days after moving in, a significant number because it is the same span of time between Jesus's crucifixion and his resurrection from the tomb. Offred's exploration of the message leads to Cora, one of the Marthas, witnessing Offred's own resurrection from what she assumes is death. Offred falls asleep in the closet and, when Cora finds her in the morning, Cora screams in terror thinking that Offred has died like the previous handmaid. Offred, unlike her predecessor, isn't dead and is able to rise and leave the closet. The hidden message itself contains the idea of rising, of resurrection—*Don't let the bastards get you down.*

Faith, Hope, and Love

In chapter 19, Offred looks at a cushion in her room embroidered with the word *faith* and thinks about the other two cushions that must be missing: "I wonder what has become of the other two cushions. There must have been three, once, HOPE and CHARITY" (110). Here, Offred thinks of a verse from the famous passage on love in 1 Corinthians: "and now abideth faith, hope, charity, these three; but the greatest of these is charity" in the King James Version or, in a more modern version, "and now these three remain: faith, hope and love. But the greatest of these is love" (1 Corinthians

44

13:13 NIV). The theocracy of Gilead provides Offred with a false faith completely devoid of hope and charity, but she still seeks faith, hope, and love. These three biblical concepts form key parts of true Christianity, as opposed to the false religion used as a front for tyranny in Gilead.

For Offred, faith, hope, and love as she experiences them while imprisoned in Gilead are primarily centered on her husband, Luke, and their daughter. Offred includes the concept of prayer in her memories of them. When she thinks about Luke and their daughter, she says, "From time to time I can see their faces, against the dark, flickering like the images of saints, in old foreign cathedrals, in the light of the drafty candles; candles you would light to pray by, kneeling, your forehead against the wooden railing, hoping for an answer" (103–4). For Offred, Luke and her daughter are her saints. This vision of Offred's saints and her veneration of her beloved "saints," Luke and her daughter, seem to lead her toward a belief of a higher sort, a form of hope. In orthodox religions, the veneration of the saints leads searchers toward a deeper belief in God. Offred's hope for Luke and for her daughter, and her association of them with prayer, seems to broaden into a yearning to believe in new life involving some kind of salvation and resurrection from the oppressive life she knows in Gilead. She also prays desperately in her memory of attempting to cross the border into Canada with her daughter and Luke: "It's going to be all right, I said, prayed in my head. Oh let it. Let us cross, let us across" (225). Her genuine prayers—desires for help and answers and an attempt at belief—contrast sharply with the false religion permeating Gilead.

Offred's struggle with faith is seen in chapter 18 when she sifts through possible fates for her missing husband. Just before Offred launches into a litany of "I believes," she decides, "It's lack of love we die from" (103). Offred repeats "I believe" over ten times in the rest of this same chapter. She imagines various possibilities for what happened to Luke. He could be lying face down, dead in a ditch. He could be imprisoned somewhere. He could have been helped to safety by the Quakers. Offred concludes the chapter with a crescendo of "I believes": "But I believe in all of them, all three versions of Luke, at one and the same time. This contradictory way of believing seems to me, right now, the only way I can believe anything. Whatever the truth is, I will be ready for it. This also is a belief of mine" (106). Offred claims to believe all three things about Luke at the same time: that he died, was imprisoned, and then "that he made it, reached the bank, swam the river, crossed the border" (105). This chapter ends with Offred riffing on hope:

One of the gravestones in the cemetery near the earliest church has an anchor on it and an hour-glass, and the words *In Hope.*

In Hope. Why did they put that above a dead person? Was it the corpse hoping, or those still alive?

Does Luke hope? (106)

As she imagines different fates for Luke and wonders how much he might hope, she struggles to have faith in his future, faith that something good happened to him and that he is somewhere and has hope.

Just as she wrangles with hope and faith, Offred also examines the concept of love. In chapter 35, after a flash-back about Luke, Offred tosses around the meaning of love in a conversation with the Commander:

Falling in love, I said. . . . It was the central thing; it was the way you understood yourself; if it never happened to you, not ever, you would be like a mutant. . . . We were falling women. We believed in it, this downward motion: so lovely, like flying. . . . *God is love*, they once said, but we reversed that, and love, like heaven, was always just around the corner." (225–26)

Offred ends this reflection on love with two lines especially significant in the context of religion and belief: "We were waiting, always, for the incarnation. That word, made flesh" (226). Here Offred quotes part of a verse from the Gospel of John: "And the Word was made flesh, and dwelt among us, (and we beheld his glory, the glory as of the only begotten of the Father,) full of grace and truth" (John 1:14). When she thinks about love, Offred conflates God's love as described in the Bible with the love she shares with people on earth, specifically in romantic relationships and specifically with Luke. In the course of the novel, she finds this form of love with Nick and in her memories of Luke. As she engages love in the novel, Offred asserts the human need for love just as she exhibits the human need to practice faith and hope.

3

Religion Gone Awry

What is needed for really good tyranny is an unquestionable idea or authority. Political disagreement is political disagreement. But political disagreement with a theocracy is heresy.

~ Margaret Atwood, *Moving Targets: Writing with Intent*

In the introduction to the Anchor Books 2017 edition of *The Handmaid's Tale*, Margaret Atwood addresses a question frequently asked about *The Handmaid's Tale*: Is it anti-religion? Atwood responds by saying, "So the book is not 'anti-religion.' It is against the use of religion as a front for tyranny; which is a different thing altogether" (xviii). *The Handmaid's Tale* brims over with examples of religion gone awry. The dystopian Republic of Gilead hides its nightmarish agenda behind the veneer of religion. It co-opts and politicizes the idea of God for its own power and purposes. Its printed propaganda includes the slogan "*God Is a National Resource*," and in Gilead, this is true (213). Religion is used to maintain the business of the republic, the nation of Gilead itself, and the power of those who lead it, not to actually practice any form of sincere faith.

Abandoned Churches

One of the early clues Atwood gives the readers that this republic is actually a dystopia using religion for political control but lacking actual faith is that churches have become museums. Although supposedly God-centered, there is never any mention of anyone going to church in this novel. In chapter 6, Offred and Ofglen pass a church while they're shopping.

> The church is a small one, one of the first erected here, hundreds of years ago. It isn't used anymore, except as a museum. Inside it you can see

50

paintings, of women in long somber dresses, their hair covered by white caps, and of upright men, darkly clothed and unsmiling. Our ancestors. Admission is free. (31)

The description of the women ancestors harkens back to the Puritans. Even though Gilead touts itself as a theocracy, it appears no one goes to church and that churches no longer even function as such. Instead of church attendance functioning as a mark of faith, inhabitants of Gilead attend ceremonies—marriages and executions—put on by the State. They can mark their piety by ordering prayers at Soul Scrolls that are printed by machines and have no human or divine element. The founders of Gilead, despite all of their righteous claims, set up a society that empties religion of its original meaning and significance but uses its holy books and systems to horrifying ends.

Subverted Beliefs

Similarly, in this upside-down theocracy, truly good characters (like Offred) are wary of "true believers"—the ones who have bought into Gilead's creepy agenda. When Offred is in the Rachel and Leah Center, she has to be careful what she says around the enthusiasts: "The Aunts walked at the head of the line and at the end, so the only danger was from the others. Some were believers and might report us" (71). Belief here refers not to a belief in God but to belief in the values and practices of Gilead. Eventually, after Offred has her assignment and gets to feel comfortable with Ofglen, Ofglen lets down her guard and tells Offred about May Day, the rebel group. For the first time, they trust each other, so they admit,

> "I thought you were a true believer," Ofglen says.
> "I thought you were," I say.
> "You were always so stinking pious."
> "So were you," I reply. I want to laugh, shout, hug her. (168)

In this self-proclaimed theocracy, things are inverted. True believers are the ones to be afraid of, those who buy into the regime's twisted creed and help enforce it. True belief refers to belief in a political system and regime, not in God.

Access to the Bible Restricted

Another clue to Gilead's use of religion as a front for tyranny is that, though Gilead claims to be a Christian nation, almost no one is allowed to read the Bible, Christianity's central text. Offred, in chapter 9, bemoans the fact that she has no access to a Bible anymore. She realizes how she took that for granted once. In a flashback of her rendezvous with Luke in a hotel, she recalls, "Careless, I was careless, in those rooms. I could lift the telephone and food would appear on a tray, food I had chosen. Food that was bad for me, no doubt, and drink. There were Bibles in the dresser drawers, put there by some charitable society, though probably no one read them very much" (51). Now, only very few have access to the Bible. Offred's Commander is one who does. He only reads the Bible to the household on the night of the Ceremony.

> He . . . fumbles with the ornate brass-bound leather-covered box that stands on the table beside the chair. He inserts the key, opens the box, lifts out the Bible, an ordinary copy, with a black cover and gold-edged pages. The Bible is kept locked up, the way people once kept tea locked up, so the servants wouldn't steal it. It's an incendiary device: who knows what we'd make of it, if we ever got our hands on it? We can be read to from it, by him, but we cannot read. (87)

Those in power in this theocracy selectively use the Bible to reinforce the need for procreation, to justify their use of the Handmaids. Offred explains, "We had it read to us every breakfast, as we sat in the high school cafeteria, eating porridge with cream and brown sugar" (88–89).

The Bible Misquoted to Manipulate

The result of taking the Bible away from almost everyone except those most powerful is that it is not just figuratively misused but also literally misquoted. Aunt Lydia is the greatest offender of misquoting the Bible. When Aunt Lydia quotes Scripture, she does so with many mistakes. Her misquotes, however, aren't accidental. She skews Bible passages in an attempt to manipulate the Handmaids into seeing things her way. When teaching her fledgling Handmaids her views about men, she explains, "Of course some of them will try. . . . All flesh is weak" (45). Offred remembers, "All flesh is grass, I corrected her in my head" (45). Here, Offred correctly quotes sections both from Isaiah, "The voice said, Cry. And he said, What shall I cry? All flesh is grass, and all the goodliness thereof is as the flower of the field'" (Isaiah 40:6), and from 1 Peter, "For all flesh is as grass, and all the glory of man as the flower of grass. The grass withereth, and the flower thereof falleth away" (1 Peter 1:24). Offred also recalls Aunt Lydia's warning about the Wives: "Try to pity them. Forgive them, for they know not what they do" (46). Here, Aunt Lydia's use of the Bible seems especially egregious because she appropriates "Forgive them, for they know not what they do," the prayer Christ prayed regarding those who executed him as he died on the cross (Luke 23:34). Aunt Lydia uses those words to encourage the Handmaids to forgive the ways they might be mistreated by the Wives. Her erroneous Bible lessons continue throughout the novel.

Those in power at the Rachel and Leah Center use the Bible as propaganda for the Handmaids in training:

> For lunch it was the Beatitudes. Blessed be this, blessed be that. They played it from a tape, so not even an Aunt would be guilty of the sin of reading. The voice was a man's. *Blessed be the poor in spirit, for theirs is the kingdom of heaven. Blessed are the merciful. Blessed be the meek. Blessed are the silent.* I knew they made that up, I knew it was wrong, and they left things out, too, but there was no way of checking. (89)

Here, we see the insidious way Gilead manipulates Bible verses for its own ends. In this case, except for the first Beatitude, which is listed in full, the taped voice only recites one half of each of the other Beatitudes, purposefully omitting the reward half.

More garbled Bible quotes appear in the birthing ceremony as Janine (Ofwarren) labors. The Handmaids recite three times: "*From each*, says the slogan, *according to her ability; to each according to his needs*." Offred muses, "It was from the Bible, or so they said, St. Paul again, in Acts" (117). The quote does not appear in the book of Acts, or the Bible, and is actually a version of a well-known statement by Karl Marx: "From each according to his ability, to each according to his needs" (from his *Critique of the Gotha Program*). Marx wrote this with an impulse toward equality. The leaders of Gilead, always looking for ways to emphasize the burden on women to please men, have twisted the slogan, reiterating how women *give* to fulfill what the men *need*. The women are giving; the men are taking. This manipulated phrase becomes the mantra Handmaids are forced to live by.

Religious-Sounding Rhetoric

The Army

The Republic of Gilead runs on religious rhetoric, or, more accurately, religious-sounding rhetoric. The ones in power use their claim of divine right as a warrant for their tyranny. Sometimes their abuse of religious language is just silly, such as the way they name their cars—Behemoth, Whirlwind, and Chariot. Slightly more unsettling is how they name their military units as angels of various sorts. Atwood writes, "The

Appalachian Highlands, says the voice-over, where the Angels of the Apocalypse, Fourth Division, are smoking out a pocket of Baptist guerillas, with air support from the Twenty-first Battalion of the Angels of Light" (82). The army of Gilead is given a divine name that suggests a protective role as opposed to a name that reveals them for what they are: a militant instrument of persecution.

The Children of Ham

A news report Offred sees on television refers to a group of people who are being resettled as "the Children of Ham" (83). In the Bible, Ham is one of the sons of Noah and the father of the nation of Canaan. In Genesis, Ham sees his father naked, and Noah curses him: "Cursed be Canaan; a servant of servants shall he be unto his brethren" (Genesis 9:25). In biblical terms, "the Children of Ham" would most likely be seen as foreigners as opposed to the people of Israel. Some groups later believed the darker-skinned races were descendants of Ham and used these verses to prop up racist agendas. The rhetoric here implies that the leaders of Gilead want their land cleansed of "the other"—of religious, political, and/or racial difference. The language "children of Ham" allows Gilead to present those it doesn't like as cursed and force them to move.

Other Religions Attacked

Another way the Republic of Gilead promotes and pre-
serves its own twisted form of religion is by continuously
working to defeat so-called rebellious religious groups who
attack them, especially the Baptists and the Quakers. The
Quakers are portrayed as especially sincere in their religious beliefs because they have formed an Underground
Femaleroad to help the Handmaids escape their enslave-
ment. They are the ones who try to help Moira when she
escapes for a while. Moira tells Offred, "One of the hardest
things was knowing that these other people were risking
their lives for you when they didn't have to. But they said
they were doing it for religious reasons and I shouldn't take
it personally. That helped some. They had silent prayers
every evening" (247). The Quakers' sincere religious beliefs
lead them to risk their lives to help others, as opposed to
Gilead using religion as a means of oppressing others.
There are other resistant religious groups, named in the
news as being defeated by Gilead's Angels or seen in the
Catholic priests and Jews left hanging dead on the Wall.
Gilead works to eliminate or manipulate individuals with
sincere faith so it can maintain control through its perverted version of religion. Only the State's form of religion
is allowed to survive.

Religious Ceremonies

Salvagings

Gilead's religious rhetoric is insidious. Its perverse ceremonies have names that sound religious, borrowing from the Judeo-Christian tradition. The first one we come across in the novel is "Salvagings." That word intentionally sounds a lot like *salvation*, a basic tenet in the Christian faith that refers to the redemption or deliverance that comes from belief in Jesus Christ. The word *salvage* refers to a rescue of some kind. But during Salvagings in *The Handmaid's Tale*, people are not rescued or offered hope; they are killed. In chapter 6, Offred comments on this ceremony: "The football stadium is that way too, where they hold the Men's Salvagings. As well as the football games. They still have those" (30–31). She and Ofglen walk on toward the Wall, where the victims of the Salvagings are hung as a kind of medieval reminder of what not to do: "There must have been a Men's Salvaging early this morning. . . . We stop, together as if on signal, and stand and look at the bodies. It doesn't matter if we look. We're supposed to look: this is what they are there for, hanging on the Wall" (32). She resists the Wall's message: "What we are supposed to feel towards these bodies is hatred and scorn. This isn't what I feel" (33). The Wall serves as a symbol of violence, a threat and warning to Gilead's citizens.

Particicution

Particicution, like Salvaging, is a combining of two words to create one new term. In this case, Particicution comes from the chilling combination of *participation* and *execution*. In this Particicution ceremony, the Handmaids are to execute an accused rapist with their bare hands. Ofglen rushes in to put him out of his misery and later whispers to Offred that he was "a political," implying that the accusations of rape were false (280). As she opens the Particicution, Aunt Lydia tells the Handmaids that the biblical penalty for rape is death and cites Deuteronomy 22:23–29 as the justification for this punishment. In a twisted use of religion, the Handmaids are told to execute an accused rapist while Gilead uses other parts of the Bible to justify the commanders raping the Handmaids.

Prayvaganzas

Prayvaganza conflates two words: *prayer* and *extravaganza*. Offred explains that Women's Prayvaganzas "are for group weddings . . . usually. The men's are for military victories"

(220). Occasionally, the women's ceremonies are also for nuns who recant their vows. The term implies prayer; however, the Prayvaganzas themselves have little to do with prayer and far more to do with propaganda and control. The language of the marriage ceremony that happens at Women's Prayvaganzas continues the manipulation of Bible verses for Gilead's political ends. After blaming women for every kind of transgression ("And Adam was not deceived, but the woman being deceived was in the transgression" [221]), the Commander declares, "Notwithstanding she shall be saved by childbearing, if they continue in faith and charity and holiness with sobriety" (221). Offred questions the odd theology of that promise and thinks, "Saved by childbearing. . . . What did we suppose would save us, in the time before?" (221). She is right to question the odd vows the young brides forcibly repeat. In their biblical context in 1 Timothy, the verses are part of Paul's instructions for worship and do not describe marriage.

During the Prayvaganza ceremony, former nuns who were found to be fertile are forced to renounce their vows of celibacy "to the common good" (220). Offred observes that they always have welts because "they don't let go easily" (221). Gilead refuses to let these women practice their sincere faith and instead forces them to participate in the religious structures concocted to preserve the men in power. Another abuse of religion connected to nun imagery is how the Handmaids are dressed like nuns in red. After comparing her room to a nunnery, Offred describes her required uniform:

> The red gloves are lying on the bed. I pick them up, pull them onto my hands, finger by finger. Everything except the wings around my face is red: the color of blood, which defines us. The skirt is ankle-length, full, gathered to a flat yoke that extends over the breasts, the sleeves are full. The white wings too are prescribed issue; they are to keep us from seeing, but also from being seen. (8)

Offred compares her clothing to blood more than once, calling herself "a Sister, dipped in blood" (9), which is fitting since her very existence depends on her fertility to produce a healthy child. Though they look like nuns, instead of being married to Christ, as celibate orthodox nuns are expected to be, these Handmaids are flesh-and-blood examples of religion gone awry. Instead of the voluntary celibacy practiced by nuns, they are raped every time they endure a Ceremony.

The Ceremony

The most crucial ceremony cloaked in the veneer of religion in Gilead is the Ceremony where the Handmaids are held by the wives and raped by the commanders. Prior to the Ceremony, the Commander reads verses selected by Gilead to justify the abuse of these women. The positions the three take during the Ceremony come from the foundational verse used as justification of the whole system of Handmaids. The verse reads, "And she said, Behold my maid Bilhah, go in unto her; and she shall bear upon my knees, that I may also have children by her" (Genesis 30:3).

Religious Practices Gone Awry

Confession

In Christianity, confession is a central practice. In the Catholic Church, confession of sins to a priest is one of the seven sacraments, or seven foundational rites by which individuals interact with God. Confession in the Christian faith can also refer to confessing belief in God and in Christ. For example, the Bible describes confession of faith in Jesus as a crucial part of the Christian faith: "That if thou shalt confess with thy mouth the Lord Jesus, and shalt believe in thine heart that God hath raised him from the dead, thou shalt be saved. For with the heart man believeth unto righteousness; and with the mouth confession is made unto salvation" (Romans 10:9–10). Gilead takes the foundational Christian practice of confession and twists it. At the Rachel and Leah Center, the trainee Handmaids are expected to attend Testifying daily. Here again, the Gilead religious rhetoric, Testifying, sounds like confession but is actually a grotesque means of shaming and controlling the Handmaids. Offred describes the experience: "It's Janine, telling about how she was gang-raped at fourteen and had an abortion. . . . At Testifying, it's safer to make things up than to say you have nothing to reveal" (71). In this convoluted "religious" practice, the Handmaids are blamed for rape. After Janine confesses her rape, the Handmaids chant in unison, "*Her* fault, *her* fault, *her* fault" until Janine finally testifies, "It was my fault, she says. It was my own fault. I led them on. I deserved the pain" (72). Late in the novel, Offred offers up a sincere confession. Chapter 41 begins with her words, "I wish this story were different. . . . I'm sorry there is so much pain in this story" (267). Nevertheless, she continues, "So I will myself to go on. I am coming to a part you will not like at all, because in it I did not behave well, but I will try nonetheless to leave nothing out" (268). Here, the reader witnesses a real confession, painful though it is, as contrasted to the false confessions and shame forced on the women in the Rachel and Leah Center.

Prayer

Citizens of Gilead, at least the ones with power, call Soul Scrolls to order prayers, a deeply impersonal, mechanized, and controlled version of prayer. Offred describes how it works:

> What the machines print is prayers, roll upon roll, prayers going out endlessly. They're ordered by Compuphone, I've overheard the Commander's Wife doing it. Ordering prayers from Soul Scrolls is supposed to be a sign of piety. . . . There are five different prayers: for health, wealth, a death, a birth, a sin. You pick the one you want, punch in the number, then punch in the number of times you want the prayer to be repeated. The machines talk as they print out the prayers; if you like, you can go inside and listen to them, the toneless metallic voices repeating the same thing over and over. . . . There are no people inside the building: the machines run by themselves. You can't hear the voices from outside; only a murmur, a hum, like a devout crowd, on its knees. (167)

Ofglen and Offred joke around and call them Holy Rollers, but Soul Scrolls' existence indicates how twisted Gilead's approach to anything remotely religious is. Conspicuously, there are no people at Soul Scrolls, only mechanical prayers ordered over the phone in order to impress someone in power. Gileadeans practice their religion, their prayers, remotely if at all. Offred and Ofglen are honest with each other; they criticize the crazy religious setup that enslaves them. Ofglen asks Offred if she believes God listens to the machines, and both women are relieved when Offred answers no. The ability to see through a religious façade instituted to maintain tyranny marks the two women as allies who can trust each other.

At the Rachel and Leah Center, Offred and the other Handmaids are encouraged to pray for specific Gileadean values: "what we prayed for was emptiness, so we would be worthy to be filled: with grace, with love, with self-denial, semen and babies" (194). These prayers are ironic: the reality of a Handmaid's role in Gilead is all about self-denial, semen, and babies, nothing about grace and love.

Communion

Another traditional religious practice that goes awry in *The Handmaid's Tale* is Communion. Communion in the Catholic and Protestant churches alike is often the centerpiece of a worship service, where believers eat the bread and drink the wine as an act of remembering Christ's sacrifice on the cross. Christ instituted the act of Communion at the Last Supper, the night before he was crucified. When the Handmaids gather to witness Janine give birth, they experience a brief hint of Communion. They are allowed to drink spiked grape juice and hold each other's hands as part of the birthing ceremony. Births are the pinnacle of religion in Gilead, a society constructed around using the bodies of women who can give birth to children. As mentioned earlier, Offred envisions how Gilead sees and uses her in a way that invokes Communion when she realizes that, to the Commander, she is more than "a chalice with no wine in it, an oven—to be crude—minus the bun" (163). To others in Gilead, then, she is valuable only for what her body can hold: a child. What the reader finds more than any kind of semblance to actual Communion is a perversion of Communion linked to using women for their potential to bear children rather than Christ's act of loving sacrifice.

Religious Music

Hymns or spirituals used for religious worship prior to Gilead are also used by the regime. For instance, at the Prayvaganza they sing the spiritual "There Is a Balm in Gilead." At another point in the novel, before one of the Ceremonies,

Offred's household has gathered to watch television, and they come to a channel where a male choir is singing "Come to the Church in the Wildwood." Here are the first four lines of this old hymn:

> There's a church in the valley in the wildwood
> No lovelier spot in the dale.
> No place is so dear to my childhood
> As the little brown church in the vale.

Before a Ceremony later in the book, Serena Joy turns the TV to a baritone singing "Whispering Hope," another gospel song.

While these songs and others like them are allowed, other hymns are not. At the beginning of chapter 10, Offred tries to remember the words to "Amazing Grace."

> Sometimes I sing to myself, in my head; something lugubrious, mournful, Presbyterian:
>
> *Amazing grace, how sweet the sound*
> *Could save a wretch like me,*
> *Who once was lost, but now am found,*
> *Was bound, but now am free.*
>
> I don't know if the words are right. I can't remember. Such songs . . . are considered too dangerous. They belong to outlawed sects. (54)

Offred does not quote the lyrics to "Amazing Grace" quite right, especially the second line of the hymn, which goes "*that* saved a wretch like me." Offred's mistaken lyric here is more fitting for her predicament because "could save" implies a future rescue of some sort, one she certainly hopes for. The outlawed sects she refers to are the Baptists, Catholics, and Lutherans, various sincerely religious groups not under the controlling thumb of Gilead.

Absence of Belief, Mercy, and Love

Belief

Gilead seems to lack any kind of sincere belief, especially by the Commanders themselves. Though they created Gilead and its laws, they seem to be the worst at following the rules they put into place. Throughout the novel, we see Offred's Commander refuse to conform to the society he helped create. He sneaks Offred into his room two or three nights a week, even though Offred says, "He knows my situation, none better. He knows all the rules" (154). Offred reminds herself "especially the Commanders . . . preach purity in all things" (165). They preach it; they do not live it. Tipsy one night, the Commander turns on the Radio Free America and grumbles about the news: "Damn Cubans, he says. All that filth about universal daycare" (209). Gilead *says* it puts family first, cares for children, begs for children, but here the Commander voices his disgust at the thought of something specifically designed to help families and children.

The Commander flaunts his hypocrisy when he dresses up Offred and takes her to Jezebel's, a nightclub/brothel where all the rules about family and purity are brazenly broken. Offred can hardly believe it:

"It's a club?" I say.

"Well, that's what we call it, among ourselves. The club."

"I thought this sort of thing was strictly forbidden," I say.

"Well, officially," he says. "But everyone's human, after all." (237)

Except the Handmaids, of course. Offred is the object of her Commander's little rebellions, dressed up, transported. She is there to be his mirror, so he can watch himself playing the part of the rebel, feasting on the forbidden. The Commander needs Offred to establish and reinforce his rebellious, unfettered persona. For Offred, conformity is survival. For him, it's a mask he can slip on and off.

Love

Another central element of Christianity missing in Gilead is love. Love has no place in this supposed theocracy, although the word *love* appears hundreds of times in the Bible. At the Rachel and Leah Center, Offred notices initials carved into her desk.

> The initials are sometimes in two sets, joined by the word *loves. J.H. loves B.P. 1954. O.R. loves L.T.* These seem to me like the inscriptions I used to read about, carved on the stone walls of caves, or drawn with a mixture of soot and animal fat. They seem to me incredibly ancient. . . . This carving, done with a pencil dug many times into the worn varnish of the desk, has the pathos of all vanished civilizations. (113)

Here Offred spells out the attitude toward love in Gilead: it's something extinct. Aunt Lydia's lessons reinforce this idea: "*Love*, said Aunt Lydia with distaste. Don't let me catch you at it. No mooning and June-ing around here, girls. Wagging her finger at us. *Love* is not the point" (220). The point of the relationships women are allowed to have, made clear here and in the wedding ceremony, is procreation and serving the needs of men, nothing else. In its absence, Offred yearns for love and talks about how she puts butter on her skin as a way of maintaining her belief that she "will some day get out . . . be touched again, in love or desire" (97). Other forms of love are also discouraged or absent—Handmaids are separated from any children they had before Gilead and from any children they bear under its rule.

The Christian faith (as opposed to the version of Christianity put forth in Gilead) believes that God loves human beings. Love holds an integral role in Christian belief and practice. In the New Testament, Jesus tells his followers that the greatest commandment is to "love the Lord thy God with all thy heart, and with all thy soul, and with all thy mind" and the second is to "love thy neighbor as thyself" (Matthew 22:37–40). Gilead strips interpersonal relationships of love and makes no mention of love as part of faith.

Mercy

Without love, it follows there is also no mercy in Gilead. It is a society founded on legalism, with rules that must be strictly followed. The Aunts' sole purpose is to make sure the Handmaids understand the rules. Eyes and Guardians watch all the citizens to be sure they follow the strictures of their positions. Therefore, instead of mercy in Gilead, there is vengeance. The Wall (as discussed above) is at the center of this republic—a marquee of vengeance with the dead bodies of those found guilty of disobedience dangling for all to see.

Religion has gone awry in Gilead. The churches are museums nobody visits. The citizens of this republic don't pray; they order their prayers from a room with computers, a room devoid of people. Those in power scoff at their own laws because "they're only human." They treat women as slaves for sex and childbirth and fail to acknowledge that they have stripped women of their lives and their humanity. There is no love, no mercy, no authentic belief. Gilead is a true dystopia using religion as a front for tyranny.

4

Gender and Politics

Whether he's making her like it or making her dislike it or making her pretend to like it is important but it's not the most important thing. The most important thing is making her. Over, from nothing, new. From scratch, the way he wants.

~ Margaret Atwood, "Iconography" in
Murder in the Dark

The Handmaid's Tale contains a panoply of abuses against women. The Gileadean regime abuses women and does so in many ways that echo past abuses of women often justified by a dangerously skewed reading of Scripture or by straightforward biblical misinterpretations. Most of the strictures set in place by those in power in Gilead are used to control women. Early on in *The Handmaid's Tale*, we discover that no woman is really free anymore. They are all trapped under strict rules and restrictions. They all wear uniforms identifying their role in this regime. None of them have careers, unless you call what the Aunts do, oppressing and abusing other women, a career. None of them have any money or any possessions they can call their own. They are all watched constantly. The Wives have a little more power than the Handmaids but are as trapped as the Handmaids in a lot of ways. Gender, politics, and religion are a dangerous combination in Gilead as those in power use their own form of religion in terrifying and chilling ways. The desire for control over women and the religious justifications for it have horrifying consequences for how woman are treated and how their lives are oppressed and shaped by those in power. Because of Gilead's desire for control and the twisted way it combines religion and politics, women in this novel are bereft, trapped, infantilized, objectified, viewed as animals, fragmented, and silenced.

In order to justify their treatment of women, the Commanders who established this republic leaned heavily on a few biblical passages that supported their extreme manifestation of traditional values. Their favorite verses, of course, involve references to handmaids early on in Genesis. They also carefully selected some verses from Paul's letters exhorting women to submit themselves. In doing this, they totally ignored and suppressed the many powerful women and their stories contained in the Bible. For instance, Deborah is a woman featured in the book of Judges. She is a prophetess and the fourth judge of Israel—a powerful woman. Under her leadership, a long-time enemy of Israel is defeated. Her full story can be read in Judges 4–5. Esther, another powerful woman, has the courage to defend her people and is victorious over those plotting the deaths of her people. There are several women in the Gospels who are some of Jesus's closest companions and who are first given the major revelations about his life and resurrection. Gilead, however, ignores these women because they wouldn't help it uphold its male dominance, and instead focuses on the religious words and ideas it can appropriate to assert its power and control.

Bereaved Women

The religious control exerted over women in Gilead causes immense pain and suffering. The Handmaids in this new regime are bereft of their old lives, their husbands, their children. Because the Commanders want to use the Handmaids' fertility to their own advantage, they take away all ties to the Handmaids so they will be completely under the Commanders' control and available to them only. Offred knows Luke, her husband, may have been killed. Those in power in Gilead have taken away her daughter and given her to a politically well-connected family. Now Offred lives a life completely controlled by her viable womb. Offred's flashbacks, especially those of her former, yearned-for family, recur frequently and serve as reminders of how much she has lost.

The Wives have also been forced to give up their old lives. They are told what to wear, what to do, where to go. For instance, Serena Joy once worked as an evangelist and television personality, first through a singing career and then as a speaker who focused on traditional family values and the need for women to stay home. Ironically, in the past, Serena Joy could travel and give speeches; now she also must stay home.

Infantilized Women

Throughout *The Handmaid's Tale* women are treated like children—infantilized. Offred remembers her training at the hands of the Aunts in what she calls the Red

Center: "Modesty is invisibility, said Aunt Lydia. Never forget it. To be seen—to be *seen*—is to be—her voice trembled—penetrated. What you must be, girls, is impenetrable. She called us girls" (28). Aunt Lydia's injunction seems to warn the grown women at the Red Center against acting the part of grown-up women, sexually aware, part of the world. She seems to be browbeating them into retreating into childhood, not only mentally but physically recapturing, somehow, their virginity—unseen, unpenetrated.

Once she gets to her assignment, Offred is treated like a child, especially by the household staff. When she asks what happened to the Commander's former Handmaid, they won't tell her. "But Rita clamped her lips together. I am like a child here, there are some things I must not be told. What you don't know won't hurt you, was all she would say" (53). Here, Rita spouts at Offred the kind of platitudes someone says to a child. It's no wonder that a bit later, Offred views herself as childlike: "I fold back the sheet, get carefully up, on silent bare feet, in my nightgown, go to the window, like a child, I want to see" (97). Later in the novel, Rita again treats Offred like a child: "'Could I have a match?' I ask her. Surprising how much like a small, begging child she makes me feel, simply by her scowl, her stolidity; how importunate and whiny" (207). Because Gilead has stripped Offred of all her freedoms and possessions, she has to ask for things like a wheedling child, and she is treated that way at meals. "I sit at the little table, eating creamed corn with a fork. I have a fork and a spoon, but never a knife. When there's meat they cut it up for me ahead of time, as if I'm lacking manual skills or teeth" (228). This description of meals accentuates how much Offred is infantilized. She's treated like a toothless baby, a child who has to have her meat cut up for her even though she is an adult capable of a full and independent life of her own.

In the birth episode, at Ofwarren's Commander's house, Offred overhears the Wives gossiping about their Handmaids. The Wives characterize their Handmaids as recalcitrant, fussed-over children:

Some of them [Handmaids], why, they aren't even clean. And won't give you a smile, mope in their rooms, don't wash their hair, the *smell*. I have to get the Marthas to do it, almost have to hold her down in the bathtub, you practically have to bribe her to get her to take a bath even, you have to threaten her.

I had to take stern measures with mine, and now she doesn't eat her dinner properly; and as for the other thing, not a nibble. (115)

The Commander infantilizes Offred, too. At one of their nightly meetings in his office, the Commander asks her what kind of black-market item she would like. She asks for hand lotion. "I think I could get some of that, he said, as if indulging a child's wish for bubble gum" (159). Similarly, at another one of their clandestine meetings, during one of their Scrabble games, the Commander lets her win. Offred notes that when he is with her in his study, "he is positively daddyish" (184). The Commander is playing the role of "daddy" to his "girl" in another twisted use of his power and authority. Later, he will literally help her play dress up when he gives her the gaudy outfit to wear to Jezebel's. The dress itself is so outlandish, it's like something a little girl would choose to dress up in: "He's holding a handful, it seems, of feathers, mauve and pink. Now he shakes this out . . . there are the cups for the breasts, covered in purple sequins. The sequins are tiny stars. The feathers are around the thigh holes" (230). When she and the Commander arrive at Jezebel's, she's astounded by the scene: "At first glance there's a cheerfulness to this scene. It's like a masquerade party; they are like oversize children, dressed up in togs they've rummaged from trunks" (235). The Gileadean regime finds ways to put all women into boxes and minimize their ability and power to do anything beyond provide sex and children.

As Offred, her fellow Handmaids, and the women at Jezebel's know, it's dangerous not to be taken seriously, not to be viewed as an equal, especially in a society that asserts its divine right to treat women this way. Gilead's founders and leaders use several Bible passages to justify their treatment of women. They mention many of these during the marriage ceremony at the Prayvaganza, as well as at the Rachel and Leah Center and before the Ceremony as they pick and choose verses that fit their ends, combining them in a new, perverted form of religion.

Objectified Women

Women in Gilead are not only infantilized but objectified as well. Handmaids no longer have their own names but instead are given the name of their Commander as a mark of his ownership. Offred is not allowed to be a person; instead she is an object or possession of Fred. Ironically, and horribly, Handmaids' survival depends on their objectification and their bodies' ability to produce, giving a chillingly literal meaning to the verse "give me children or else I die." In its original biblical context, Rachel speaks this line to her husband Jacob out of grief at her inability to bear children: "and when Rachel saw that she bare Jacob no children, Rachel envied her sister; and said unto

Jacob, Give me children, or else I die" (Genesis 30:1–2). In Gilead, the verse has a viciously literal meaning as Handmaids are given three postings to produce children and are then discarded if they are unable to become pregnant and give birth.

Once Offred and the Commander begin to interact outside of the Ceremony, Offred is upset because the Commander *doesn't* treat her like a thing; he tries to touch her face, and it frightens her. "You could get me transferred, I said. To the Colonies. You know that. Or worse. I thought he should continue to act, in public, as if I were a large vase or a window: part of the background, inanimate or transparent" (162). If Serena Joy notices a change in their relationship, she has the power to harm Offred. Offred's survival depends on the Commander's objectification of her, especially during the Ceremonies.

Offred first feels objectified in her old life when the founders of Gilead begin to take over and enforce their misogynist policies. When her job and her money are taken from her, Offred worries that Luke "doesn't mind it at all. Maybe he even likes it. We are not each other's, anymore. Instead, I am his" (182). But it's the Commander who objectifies her continually. For instance, before they get to Jezebel's, he literally tags her: "'Here,' the Commander says. He slips around my wrist a tag, purple, on an elastic band, like the tags for airport luggage. 'If anyone asks you, say you're an evening rental,' he says" (233). Ironically, a few pages later, when Offred wonders about what they're doing at Jezebel's, because it's so very forbidden, he says, "Well, officially. . . . But everyone's human after all" (237). What he really means is: well, men are human after all. The reader isn't surprised when Offred doesn't "reply to this. I am getting fed up with him" (237).

Of course, the overriding way women are objectified in Gilead is that they are literally classified by the viability of their reproduction system, specifically their wombs. In Gilead, Handmaids are not viewed as fully human; they serve no purpose other than procreation. Offred tells us she longs to be viewed as more than a valuable resource for her potential to become pregnant. All women, not just Handmaids, are objectified and reduced to their functions: the Wives exist to stay home and hopefully become mothers to the children the Handmaids give birth to; the Marthas exist for the purpose of household duties; the Econowives for providing services to men with lower status in the new regime. Women who do not fit into these roles are dehumanized, referred to as "unwomen," and sent to work to their deaths in the Colonies.

Women as Animals

Closely aligned with the objectification of women, because both approaches treat women as less than human, is viewing them as animals. Aunt Lydia and others who exert control over the Handmaids often describe them, and treat them, like animals: "You're getting the best, you know, said Aunt Lydia. There's a war on, things are rationed. You are spoiled girls, she twinkled, as if rebuking a kitten. Naughty puss" (89). This idea of the Handmaids being pampered conflates the infantilization discussed above with the animal metaphors applied to women. Offred realizes that she is treated like an animal in a few places in the novel. For instance, she bemoans how much time she spends just waiting around. "I wait, washed, brushed, fed, like a prize pig" (69). Perhaps she thinks of that image because during one of her lectures, Aunt Lydia reminds the Handmaids: "But we can't be greedy pigs and demand too much before it's ready, now can we?" (163). The pig image describes Handmaids as animals valuable for what their bodies produce and for nothing else.

Later in the novel, Offred compares Ofglen and herself to animals because of the ways they are controlled and contained: "Now and again we vary the route; there's nothing against it, as long as we stay within the barriers. A rat in a maze is free to go anywhere, as long as it stays inside the maze" (165). Like rats in a maze, Offred and Ofglen are able to perform a certain number of actions and take a certain number of paths, rather than exist as free human beings.

The first time she sneaks into the Commander's office at night, Offred imagines how the Commander views her as an animal: "He smiles. The smile is not sinister or predatory. It's merely a smile . . . a little distant, as if I'm a kitten in a window. One he's looking at but doesn't intend to buy" (138). Offred recognizes that the Commander views her as someone who is less than human and who exists for his purposes and pleasure. In a later scene in the Commander's office, Offred imagines that he views her as his pet: "'I'll give it to you,' he says. He smiles. The Commander likes it when I distinguish myself, show precocity, like an attentive pet, prick-eared and eager to perform" (183–84).

A darkly funny woman-as-animal scene takes place in Jezebel's when Offred first sees Moira. Offred realizes Moira is still alive, but then she notices what she's wearing:

There's a wad of cotton attached to the back, I can see it as she half turns; it looks like a sanitary pad that's been popped like a piece of popcorn. I realize that it's supposed to be a tail. Attached to her head are two ears, of a rabbit or deer, it's not easy to tell; one of the ears has lost its starch of wiring and is flopping halfway down. . . . The whole costume, antique and bizarre, reminds me of something from the past, but I can't think what. A stage play, a musical comedy? (239)

Along with the humor that comes with the ridiculousness of the costume, there's a total disconnect for Offred seeing Moira dressed in a bizarre animal costume because she knows Moira from before, as a free woman and strong feminist. Seeing her as a kind of worn-down Velveteen Rabbit in a nightclub shocks Offred. When she's alone with the Commander in a hotel room at Jezebel's, Offred, again, can only think of herself as an animal: petted, branded, fettered, owned: "He's stroking my body now . . . cat stroke along the left flank, down the left leg. He stops at the foot, his fingers encircling the ankle briefly, like a bracelet, where the tattoo is, a Braille he can read, a cattle brand. It means ownership" (254). His hand encircling her ankle is very much like a handcuff or manacle asserting his ownership of Offred.

Women are encouraged to treat each other in dehumanizing ways. The Wives are complicit in the rape of the Handmaids as they literally hold a Handmaid in place during the Ceremony. Wives are also allowed to hit the Handmaids, as there is supposedly scriptural precedent. Most likely, Gilead takes this precedent from Genesis 16:6 NIV, which states that "Sarai mistreated Hagar" after Hagar became pregnant by Sarah's husband, Abraham. At the Rachel and Leah Center, when Janine (Ofwarren) is made to stand in front of the classroom for testifying, she is described as looking "disgusting: weak, squirmy, blotchy, pink, like a newborn mouse" (72). The other Handmaids, who aren't fond of Janine anyway, chant, "Crybaby. Crybaby. Crybaby" (72). The Aunts encourage the Handmaids to view each other in dehumanized ways, to treat each other with scorn, and to make each other feel shame.

The Handmaids are literally herded like cows. The Aunts keep their trainee Handmaids in line as if they are animals by controlling them with cattle prods. In turn, Offred tends to view the Aunts, especially Aunt Lydia, as animals. Offred remembers a time at the Rachel and Leah Center when she found herself staring at Aunt Lydia's mouth: "Her mouth trembled, around her front teeth, teeth that stuck out a little and were long and yellowish, and I thought about the dead mice we would find on our doorstep" (55). And a couple lines later, Offred describes Aunt Lydia pressing "her hand over her mouth of a dead rodent" (55). The reader can't help but cheer on Offred's less-than-kind descriptions comparing Aunt Lydia to animals as Aunt Lydia is one of the more despicable antagonists in the book. Offred, imprisoned and tormented by Aunt Lydia and the other Aunts, does not see these women who abuse and control other women as fully human, either.

Fragmented Women

Women in Gilead are fragmented, viewed not as full human beings but only as wombs able, or not, to conceive and bear children. Women as a group are also fragmented—encouraged to abuse and control each other. When Offred goes for her doctor visit, she describes this fragmentation: "When I'm naked I lie down on the examining table, on the sheet of chilly crackling disposable paper. I pull the second sheet, the cloth one, up over my body. At neck level there's another sheet, suspended from the ceiling. It intersects me so the doctor will never see my face. He deals with a torso only" (60). She is shocked that he offers to help with what he considers "her problem." The doctor tells her, "'Most of those old guys can't make it anymore.... Or they're sterile.' I almost gasp: he's said a forbidden word. *Sterile*. There is no such thing as a sterile man anymore, not officially. There are only women who are fruitful and women who are barren, that's the law" (61). In this dystopia, women are not only fragmented but also solely blamed for the ability or inability to bear children.

An even crueler way the Handmaids are fragmented is the way they are physically fragmented—tortured and killed—for resisting Gilead's oppressive rule. Handmaids and Wives are executed for infractions, as is anyone suspected of working with or for the resistance. Offred records that a woman's hand is cut off for reading and that Handmaids can also be executed for "unchastity" or attempting to kill their Commanders, and Wives are primarily executed for killing Handmaids, adultery, or attempting escape (275). After Moira is recaptured, the Aunts beat her feet until they no longer resemble feet: "Her feet did not look like feet at all. They looked like drowned feet, swollen and boneless, except for the color. They looked like lungs" (91). And just before that, Offred explains the logic in their cruelty: "It was the feet they'd do, for a first offense. They used steel cables, frayed at the ends. After that the hands. They didn't care what they did to your feet or your hands, even if it was permanent. Remember, said Aunt Lydia. For our purposes your feet and your hands are not essential" (91).

Offred is forced to fragment herself in order to survive the monthly rape of the Ceremony. She detaches herself from her own humanity in order to make it through. As she tells us, "one detaches oneself. One describes" (95). Just as the doctor deals only in her body, Offred is forced to separate herself from her body in order to survive repeated trauma. The previous Handmaid in Offred's house killed herself, forced by Gilead and her trauma to literally fragment life from her body. The novel's Ofglen also does this, killing herself before the Eyes take her away for probable torture and execution.

Silenced Women

Gilead silences women and makes them speechless. Toward the end of the novel, Offred, not just the Handmaid but also the recorder/writer of the story, turns to the audience and apologizes: "I'm sorry there is so much pain in this story. I'm sorry it's in fragments, like a body caught in crossfire or pulled apart by force. But there is nothing I can do to change it" (267). Here we see Offred resisting being fragmented and silenced. There are, however, many instances of silenced women in this novel. Offred describes the Rachel and Leah Center where the trainee Handmaids had to try to sleep "in the army cots that had been set up in rows, with spaces between so we could not talk" (4). Later in the novel, the Commander silences Offred when they arrive at Jezebel's. "All you have to do, I tell myself, is keep your mouth shut and look stupid. It shouldn't be that hard. The Commander does the talking for me" (236).

The altered Beatitudes the Handmaids are forced to listen to at the Rachel and Leah Center adds a Beatitude not found in the Bible: "*Blessed are the merciful. Blessed be the meek. Blessed are the silent.* I knew they made that up" (89). Tellingly, the new Gileadean Beatitude commands the Handmaids to silence. Their propaganda insinuates that silence will somehow bless the one silenced rather than oppress and enslave them.

The Handmaids aren't the only ones silenced in Gilead. The Wives are silenced as well. We see this most clearly in Serena Joy. Serena Joy, before the establishment of this new government, had been a celebrated speaker. Though she helped establish this new government and spread its message of women staying in the home, she is now the victim of its silencing too. She's trapped in a patriarchy that is partly of her own making. Offred remembers Serena Joy from the time before: "She was good at it. Her speeches were about the sanctity of home, about how women should stay home. Serena Joy didn't do this herself, she made speeches instead, but she presented this failure of hers as a sacrifice she was making for the good of all" (45). Now, Serena Joy *is* a sacrifice, silenced, trapped in the home, restricted, and forbidden to say one word against it.

Another chilling example of the silencing of women in *The Handmaid's Tale* is the disappearance or death of the feminists of Offred's mother's generation. She hopes her mother, who has been sent to the Colonies, is still alive, although Offred knows it's a death sentence to be exiled there since their job is to clean up toxic waste. Offred's mother was an outspoken feminist who marched for women's rights along with others who shared her convictions and determination, but now she is no more. Offred remembers her mother trying to warn her, "You young people don't appreciate things, she'd say. You don't know what we had to go through, just to get you where you are. Look at him [Luke, Offred's husband], slicing carrots. Don't you know how many women's lives, how many women's *bodies*, the tanks had to roll over just to get this far?" (121). In vain, Offred yearns to be able to speak to her mother though both of them have been silenced: "Mother, I think. Wherever you may be. Can you hear me?" (127).

Importantly, Offred, in the midst of all the silencing she endures, claims her own story. The book is called, after all, *The Handmaid's Tale*. It is her story to tell. Early on in the novel, at the end of chapter 7, Offred muses:

> I would like to believe this is a story I'm telling. I need to believe it. I must believe it. Those who can believe that such stories are only stories have a better chance. . . .

> Tell, rather than write, because I have nothing
> to write with. . . . But if it's a story, even in my head,
> I must be telling it to someone. You don't tell a story
> only to yourself. There's always someone else. . . .
>
> A story is like a letter. *Dear You*, I'll say. Just
> *you*, without a name. (39–40)

Offred here claims the power to share, to speak, what has happened to her despite the regime's attempts to silence her and others like her.

Unfortunately, in the aptly named *Handmaid's Tale*, the novel doesn't end with the story Offred tells but goes on to include a Historical Notes section, where scholars, years later, wrangle with her story. The scholars discussing Offred's story are sexist in their attitudes and remarks. After comparing it to Geoffrey Chaucer's work with its echo of the title *The Canterbury Tales*, Professor Pieixoto denigrates the title *The Handmaid's Tale*. He claims it was actually Professor Wade who called the manuscript that: "Those of you who know Professor Wade informally, as I do, will understand when I say that I am sure all puns were intentional, particularly that having to do with the archaic vulgar signification of the word *tail*; that being, to some extent, the bone, as it were of contention" (301). The proceedings go on to undercut Offred's narration as, at best, doubtful. They criticize her storytelling ability, if they even credit it at all: "She could have told us much about the workings of the Gileadean empire, had she the instincts of a reporter or a spy" (310). These scholars have set themselves up as the authorities who will authenticate Offred's tale, *her* story, *her* letter to the world. Atwood gives us unsubtle hints about how to read these Historical Notes and reminds us of the dangers of silencing these women and their stories. The sexism of Gilead lasts well beyond its fall, as we see when Pieixoto tells his audience to "be cautious about passing moral judgment upon the Gileadeans" (302).

The manipulative, extreme fundamentalism of the dystopian Gilead is a nightmare for everyone, especially for the women subjugated and enslaved by its supposedly religious, supposedly biblical laws and structures. As hearers of Offred's story and viewers of Gilead's horrific oppression, we of course pass moral judgment upon those who created Gilead and enforced its laws.

In the introduction to the 2017 Anchor Books edition of *The Handmaid's Tale*, Atwood addresses the issue of feminism. She writes that there are three questions readers often ask her. "First, is *The Handmaid's Tale* a 'feminist' novel?" And she goes on to answer it this way:

> If you mean an ideological tract in which all women
> are angels and/or so victimized they are incapable

of moral choice, no. If you mean a novel in which women are human beings—with all the variety of character and behavior that implies—and are also interesting and important, and what happens to them is crucial to the theme, structure, and plot of the book, then yes. (xvi)

The women in Gilead, far from the dehumanized way the theocracy treats them, are important human beings whose voices must be heard.

5

The Handmaid's Tale on TV

I remember a television program I once saw. . . . I must have been seven or eight, too young to understand it. It was the sort of thing my mother liked to watch: historical, educational. She tried to explain it to me afterwards, to tell me that the things in it had really happened, but to me it was only a story. I thought someone had made it up. I suppose all children think that, about any history before their own. If it's only a story, it becomes less frightening.

~ Margaret Atwood, *The Handmaid's Tale*

The Hulu series has taken Margaret Atwood's most famous novel and garnered an even broader audience for this unforgettable story. While season 1 follows the novel fairly closely, season 2 carries the story beyond the bounds of the narrative told in the novel. The series both engages and expands Atwood's use of religion, repeating her allusions and references and bringing in new religious and biblical elements. While each episode is so inundated with religious language, references, and moments that listing each instance would take a book far longer than this one, this chapter explores significant names, references, and themes to offer a highlight reel of how religion appears—and goes awry—in the Gilead found on television.

Names

The Hulu series begins with an emphasis on names. After the opening flashback of her escape, we see Offred sitting in her room in the Commander's house, listing furnishings because "thinking can hurt your chances." She remembers she can't even say her name—"so many things forbidden now." She may be forbidden from saying her name, but the series tells us more about her names and the names of other characters and adds new characters with significant names of their own.

June

In the series, we learn that Offred's name is June. Margaret Atwood addresses this addition in the introduction to the 2017 Anchor Books edition of the novel where she writes, "Some have deduced that Offred's real name is June, since, of all the names whispered among the Handmaids in the gymnasium/dormitory, June is the only one that never appears again. That was not my original thought, but it fits, so readers are welcome to it if they wish" (xv).

Aunt Lydia draws a religious connection between the names June and Offred in season 2, episode 4 ("Other Women"). Aunt Lydia disciplines and threatens the recaptured Offred by taking her to the Wall to see a man hanging there, the one who helped her try to escape. Aunt Lydia tells Offred, "Such a selfish girl. Who killed him?" Offred replies, "My fault." Aunt Lydia asks her, "Why did God allow such a terrible thing to happen?" Offred replies, "To teach me a lesson." At that point, Aunt Lydia corrects her. "To teach *June* a lesson. June consorted with terrorists—not Offred. Offred is free—free of blame. Offred doesn't have to bear June's guilt." Aunt Lydia sets up a dichotomy: an old, sinful June, but a new, unblemished Offred. This is reminiscent of biblical characters whose name change indicates a change in their whole identity. For example, the apostle Paul (the author of several books of the New Testament) originally appears in the Bible as Saul, a persecutor of Christians. As Saul, he actively arrests and participates in the violent persecution of Christians. After a powerful conversion experience on the road to Damascus, he becomes a Christian and changes his name to Paul. Following this logic, Aunt Lydia wrongly implies that Gilead has not deprived Offred of her old name and the life that went with it but instead has elevated her to a saintlier existence, offering her absolution and salvation.

Hannah

Along with Offred's first and last names, her daughter is given the first name Hannah. Hannah is a biblical name connected to infertility and childbirth, two important themes in *The Handmaid's Tale*. The first two chapters of 1 Samuel tell Hannah's story. Though she longs for a child, she is infertile, so she goes to the temple and prays to have a child. In her prayer, Hannah vows that if God will give her a son, she will devote him to the Lord. She and her husband Elkanah have a son they name Samuel. When he is a year old, Hannah gives him to the temple to work in God's service. We can see the many lines of connection here: a woman overcoming infertility, conceiving a child, then giving that child up. Offred's daughter's story parallels this story in Samuel because she is given up, in Gilead's eyes, for a greater good. The difference, of course, is that Hannah of the Bible willingly chooses to give up Samuel to serve God; whereas in *The Handmaid's Tale* Hannah is forcibly taken away from Offred to fulfill the hunger for children in the new regime.

Hannah's new family renames her Agnes. The name Agnes derives from the Christian saint Agnes, who was martyred under Emperor Diocletian. Saint Agnes is often pictured with a lamb. The lamb image, in terms of Christian iconography, evokes the idea of sacrifice, and Hannah, Offred's daughter, is sacrificed to the ideals of the new state.

Eden

Eden, the very young wife married to Nick in season 2, bears a name with obvious biblical connections. The Hebrew name Eden means *delight*. The biblical garden of Eden is an earthly paradise where Adam and Eve are placed at creation to walk in complete, unspoiled union with God and with each other. The biblical garden of Eden is a place of innocence and purity; however, it is also the setting for the fall. With the fall comes the curse on Adam and Eve and their expulsion from the garden of Eden. Adam's sin and curse are not mentioned in Gilead, but Eve's curse appears in some Gileadean religious ceremonies because it can be used to enforce Gilead's message that men are superior to women. God's curse on Eve, with a special emphasis on childbearing, also reinforces Gilead's message of patriarchal authority:

> To the woman he said,
> "I will make your pains in childbearing very severe;
> with painful labor you will give birth to children.
> Your desire will be for your husband,
> and he will rule over you." (Genesis 3:16 NIV)

Isaac

Eden's love interest is Isaac, and his name, like hers, entwines innocence and death (sacrifice). The biblical Isaac is the promised son born to the patriarch Abraham and his wife Sarah in their old age. In Genesis 22, God tests Abraham by telling him to take Isaac to the top of a mountain and sacrifice him as a burnt offering. Abraham obeys God's command, takes Isaac up a mountain, ties him up, and lays him on an altar. As Abraham raises the knife, preparing to slit Isaac's throat and offer him up as a sacrifice, an angel speaks to Abraham and tells him not to kill Isaac. A ram appears nearby, sent by God for Abraham to kill instead of Isaac. Isaac, saved from sacrifice, goes on to become the father of Jacob and thereby one of the patriarchs from whom the twelve sons of Jacob and the twelve tribes of Israel descend. In a society whose founders call themselves the Sons of Jacob, and who rely heavily on the Old Testament, Isaac is also a name signifying the power and status that Isaac has before his relationship with Eden.

Leah

Leah, wife of a Commander and friend of Serena Joy, appears in the series as a recurring character. Her husband has a Handmaid as well, which makes her name a fitting one. The Handmaid system comes in part from Leah in the Bible. Genesis tells the story of Rachel and Leah, sisters married to Jacob (son of Isaac). Leah gives birth to four sons, but when she experiences a period of infertility, "took Zilpah her maid, and gave her Jacob to wife" (Genesis 30:9), as her sister Rachel had done with her own slave Bilhah in an effort to have more children.

Aunt Pauline

Aunt Pauline appears in the series as an Aunt who oversees the unwomen in the Colonies. Her name aligns her with Paul, the writer of several books of the Bible's New

Testament. Many passages authored by Paul have been used—and misused—to denigrate women. For example, Ephesians 5:23 says, "For the husband is the head of the wife, even as Christ is the head of the church: and he is the savior of the body," and 1 Corinthians 14:34–35: "Let your women keep silence in the churches: for it is not permitted unto them to speak; but they are commanded to be under obedience as also saith the law. And if they will learn any thing, let them ask their husbands at home: for it is a shame for women to speak in the church."

Biblical Allusions, References, and Abuses

Punishment

Even though season 1 of the Hulu series follows the novel fairly closely, the screenwriters add even more atrocities committed in the name of Gilead's religion. Both seasons overflow with religious rhetoric as, oftentimes, the ones in power in Gilead mask their various cruelties with religious phrases or justifications. In the pilot episode, when the Commander and Offred are playing Scrabble, the camera zooms in on the word *judges*. This might be a reference to the book of the Bible by that name or to the idea of judgment, both of which hint at how legalistic Gilead is. The TV series especially depicts harsh, explicitly biblical punishments. Gilead adopts the retributive, violent forms of justice most commonly found in the Old Testament. It is seemingly prophetic when, in season 1, episode 1 ("Offred"), Offred adds to Aunt Lydia's pontificating the Beatitude, "Blessed are the meek" by murmuring, "Blessed are the ones who suffer for righteousness." This scene changes Offred's response in the novel, where she wonders why Aunt Lydia doesn't mention inheriting the earth as well. In the Hulu series especially, there seems to be an emphasis on suffering for the sake of what Gilead defines as "righteousness," even more so than in the novel. For example, in one of the opening scenes of season 1, episode 1 ("Offred"), Aunt Lydia says, "Blessed are the meek" right before she tases a rebellious Handmaid. In season 1, episode 5 ("Faithful"), Ofglen is sent to a Redemption Center, where she is forced to have a clitorectomy. Season 1, episode 9 ("The Bridge"), opens with Ofwarren (Janine) handing over her baby. When she comes out of the house with her suitcase, everyone shouts, "Praise be!" after she has just been forced to give up her child.

Commander Putnam's Adultery

When Commander Warren Putnam is on trial for adultery, his wife insists he receive the harshest punishment, so they cut off his left arm below the elbow. This harks back to the biblical injunction of "an eye for an eye," which appears in Exodus 21:22–25:

> If men strive, and hurt a woman with child, so that her fruit depart from her, and yet no mischief follow: he shall be surely punished, according as the woman's husband will lay upon him; and he shall pay as the judges determine. And if any mischief follow, then thou shalt give life for life, eye for eye, tooth for tooth, hand for hand, foot for foot, burning for burning, wound for wound, stripe for stripe.

Commander Putnam's punishment originates in the book of Matthew, which talks about cutting off a hand as a punishment for adultery:

> But I say unto you, that whosoever looketh on a woman to lust after her hath committed adultery with her already in his heart. And if thy right eye offend thee, pluck it out, and cast it from thee: for it is profitable for thee that one of thy members should perish, and not that thy whole body should be cast into hell. And if thy right hand offend thee, cut it off, and cast it from thee: for it is profitable for thee that one of thy members should perish, and

not that thy whole body should be cast into hell. (Matthew 5:28–30)

Serena Joy's Beating

Another biblically justified punishment occurs in season 2, episode 8 ("Women's Work"), when the Commander comes home from the hospital and finds out Serena Joy has been forging his signatures on important documents. He takes off his belt and beats her with it, misquoting Ephesians and combining it with other parts of the Bible while he does:

> Now we must make amends. Wives submit your-selves unto your husbands as unto the Lord. Ye husbands dwell with them according to knowledge given honor unto the life as unto the weaker vessel. But if we confess our sins . . . he is faithful and just to forgive us.

Ephesians 5 states

> Wives, submit yourselves unto your own husbands, as unto the Lord. For the husband is the head of the wife, even as Christ is the head of the church: and he is the savior of the body. Therefore as the church is subject unto Christ, so let the wives be to

their own husbands in every thing. Husbands, love
your wives, even as Christ also loved the church,
and gave himself for it. (Ephesians 5:22–25)

It does not include the phrase "now we must make amends"
or the description of "the weaker vessel" or the description
of forgiveness. The vessel description comes from 1 Peter
3:7: "Likewise, ye husbands, dwell with them according to
knowledge, giving honour unto the wife, as unto the weaker
vessel, and as being heirs together of the grace of life; that
your prayers be not hindered." The phrase about confession
of sins comes from 1 John 1:9, "If we confess our sins, he
is faithful and just to forgive us our sins and to cleanse us
from all unrighteousness," and in its biblical context does
not refer to marriage or to husbands and wives. The way
the Commander takes parts of these verses and puts them
together as one passage allows him to present himself as a
superior being with the right to beat his wife, but tellingly
he omits the parts of the verse that command husbands to
love and sacrifice themselves for their wives.

Eden and Isaac's Execution

In season 2, episode 12 ("Postpartum"), the judge sentences
Eden and Isaac to "the common mercy of the state," which

ironically means death. He uses Scripture to justify that decision. The judge cites 1 John 1:9, "If we confess our sins, he is faithful and just . . . to cleanse us from all unrighteousness." Simultaneously, and in a kind of defiance we rarely see in Eden, she quotes from a famous Corinthians chapter on love, which lists many positive and selfless qualities of love: "Love is patient. Love is kind" (1 Corinthians 13:4). The judge says, "By his hand," as Eden and Isaac are pushed into the water to drown, implying that their murder is the will of God.

Before they arrest Eden, Nick asks her to forgive him. She replies, "Let's forgive each other. The Lord said, 'When thou passeth through the waters I shall be with thee and through the river . . . when thou walkest through the fire thou shall not be burnt.'" Eden accurately quotes the King James Version of Isaiah 43:2 here, demonstrating her knowledge of what the Bible actually says. Here and when she quotes from 1 Corinthians 13, Eden's sincere and accurate recitations of Bible verses remind Gilead that their version of Christianity is false and leaves out the central elements of love and forgiveness.

Janine's Stoning

At the end of season 1, episode 10 ("Night"), there is a Salvaging to condemn Ofwarren (Janine) for trying to take her baby away from Commander Putnam and his wife and threatening to kill her child, but the Handmaids, led by Ofglen and Offred, rebel. They are supposed to stone Ofwarren to death, but they all drop their stones and walk away, saying, "Sorry, Aunt Lydia." Stoning appears as a punishment in several places in the Bible, and this particular form of punishment fits Gilead's style of taking things out of the Bible that they deem useful as ways to oppress and terrorize others.

The Noose

In season 2, episode 1 ("June"), the Handmaids head into a stadium filled with nooses. Aunt Lydia stages a fake hanging to frighten them, then sanctimoniously quotes a famous Bible verse: "You will love the Lord with all your heart." Astoundingly, she punishes them for not being willing to kill for her and then uses a verse on love to justify that punishment. The commandment to love God with all your heart appears multiple places in the Bible. It is the first of the Ten Commandments given in Deuteronomy, "and thou shalt love the Lord thy God with all thine heart, and with all thy soul, and with all thy might" (Deuteronomy 6:5). It also appears in the New Testament. Jesus, when asked by religious leaders which commandment in the law is the greatest, replies, "Thou shalt love the Lord thy God with all thy heart, and with all thy soul, and with all thy mind" (Matthew 22:37) and that it is followed by the command to love your neighbor as yourself, which is certainly never mentioned in Gilead. A similar version of this story, with a similar response by Jesus, appears in Mark 12:28–31.

Unwomen

The TV series elaborates much more on the Colonies and the unwomen exiled there. In season 2, episode 2 ("Unwomen"), the Aunts there make the unwomen kneel and pray, "Let us sing unto the Lord and pray. The Lord is Great; he is merciful. The sinners and the whores are blessed with his grace. May he bless us with his mercy forever and ever." Aunt Lydia gives a slide-show lecture in the next episode ("Baggage"). She shows the unwomen working in the Colonies and pronounces to her audience, "He will surely bless us with abundances!" Ironically, the Aunts force women being worked to death to speak of their imprisonment as mercy, grace, and abundance while the Aunts and those who send the women to the Colonies refuse to act with mercy and grace.

Women and Religion

Handmaids

BLESSED BE THE FRUIT

In the novel and the series, characters greet each other with the biblical phrase "Blessed be the fruit." Aunt Lydia greets the Handmaids that way, and they greet each other with the same phrase. This phrase comes from a significant scene in the Bible, when Mary, the pregnant mother of Jesus, visits her pregnant cousin Elizabeth, and Elizabeth greets her with these famous words:

> And she [Elizabeth] spake out with a loud voice, and said, Blessed art thou among women, and blessed is the fruit of thy womb. And whence is this to me, that the mother of my Lord should come to me? For, lo, as soon as the voice of thy salutation sounded in mine ears, the babe leaped in my womb for joy. And blessed is she that believed: for there shall be a performance of those things which were told her from the Lord. (Luke 1:42–45)

Mary's response to Elizabeth is, "For he hath regarded the low estate of his handmaiden: for, behold, from henceforth all generations shall call me blessed" (Luke 1:48).

The Hulu series leaves out a significant part of that famous phrase, "of thy womb." Those in power in Gilead—the Commanders and the Aunts—construct the biblical phrase so that it blesses the fruit, the offspring, they long for but disregards and discounts the wombs that provide those offspring. This contrasts with the passage in Luke that praises Mary as the one chosen to bear God's son.

Legalized Rape

One of the worst incidents of the Commander's use of religious rhetoric, and cruelest, is when he (and Serena Joy) rape full-term Offred to try to make her go into labor, and as they do, he quotes Scripture. It's hard to hear in the midst of Offred begging them to stop, but the Commander quotes Genesis 30, when Rachel asks Jacob to give her children through her handmaid Bilhah: "And she said, 'Behold my maid Bilhah, go in unto her; and she shall bear upon my knees, that I may also have children by her.' And she gave him Bilhah her handmaid to wife: and Jacob went in unto her" (Genesis 30:3–4 KJV). As the Commander rapes the pregnant Offred in season 2, episode 10 ("The Last Ceremony") he recites the biblical passage from Genesis used to justify the Handmaid system, which tells the story of Rachel and Bilhah. "And she said, 'Behold my handmaid, Bilhah. Go in unto her. And she shall bear upon my knees that I may also have children by her.' And she gave him her handmaid to wife, and Jacob went in unto her." Here, he uses this passage as a justification for his rape of Offred.

EVEN IN CANADA

In season 2, episode 9 ("Smart Power"), the use of religious rhetoric continues when, in Canada, the Commander is confronted by Luke, June's husband, who shouts, "You raped my wife! You remember my face because I'll remember yours." The Commander replies with a ridiculous, trivializing pun, "You should remember Scripture . . . his kingdom endures forever." This is a truncated version of several verses across the Bible that refer to God's eternal kingdom. For instance, in the Old Testament, the prophet Nathan assures King David of Israel that God promises to establish the throne of David forever: "Your house and your kingdom will endure forever before me; your throne will be established forever" (2 Samuel 7:16 NIV). The eternal kingdom here refers to God's eternal kingdom, as Jesus Christ was born as a descendant of David. The eternal kingdom also appears in the New Testament. For example, Luke 1:32–33, describing Jesus Christ, reads, "He shall be great, and shall be called the Son of Highest: and the Lord God shall give unto him the throne of his father David: And he shall reign over the house of Jacob for ever; and of his kingdom there shall be no end." Warning June's husband to watch out, the Commander claims to be one of God's chosen rulers.

Mothers and Children

Many biblical references in the series surround the Handmaids and the children they bear. The ceremony in which Janine/Ofwarren gives up her newborn daughter, Charlotte, to her Commander's wife includes a typical use of the Bible in Gilead: combining several biblical verses and phrases in order to create the biblical justification for tyranny and abuse. The ceremony includes a supposed Bible passage that reads, "For he hath regarded the low estate of his handmaiden. For, behold, from henceforth, all generations shall call me blessed. Then the handmaidens came near, they and their children. And they bowed themselves. May the Lord now show you kindness and faithfulness, and I, too, will show you the same favor. The Lord bless thee, and keep thee." This exact passage is not found in the Bible but is made up of parts of Bible verses taken from different books of the Bible and put together in a passage that serves Gilead's ends. The first line comes from Mary's song of praise to God after she learns that she will be the mother of Jesus: "And Mary said, My soul doth magnify the Lord, and my spirit hath rejoiced in God my Savior. For he hath regarded the low estate of his handmaiden: for, behold, from henceforth all generations shall call me blessed" (Luke 1:46–48). It does not have anything to do with Rachel and Leah or the scriptural precedent for Handmaids but instead comes from a mother rejoicing in her pregnancy.

The second part of the passage comes from Genesis and the story of Jacob's reunion with his brother Esau. After Jacob takes his family and possessions and leaves the house of his father-in-law, Laban (see chapter 1 for more of the story), he seeks a reunion with his brother Esau but is very afraid of his brother. When Jacob and Esau meet, Esau embraces Jacob and rejoices in their reunion. According to Genesis 33, Esau asks Jacob, "Who are those with thee?" and when Jacob tells Esau they are his children, "then the handmaidens came near, they and their children, and they bowed themselves" (Genesis 33:5–6). Biblically, it is a story of reunion and greeting, not of women surrendering their children to others. The final line references 2 Samuel 2:6 NIV ("May the Lord now show you kindness and faithfulness, and I too will show you the same favor because you have done this") and Numbers 6:24 ("The Lord bless thee, and keep thee").

In the circle ceremony in season 2, episode 4 ("Other Women"), Serena Joy and Offred stand in the center of the circle, their hands tied to each other's. There's a call-and-response use of Scripture. Serena Joy says, "Behold he who does great and unsearchable things," which seems to come from the book of Job: "Which doeth great things and unsearchable; marvellous things without number" (Job 5:9). Then the other Wives and Handmaids respond, "Wonders without number" (the second part of the verse above). Serena Joy then recites, "Let the little children come unto me" and the Wives and Handmaids respond, "For of such is the kingdom of heaven" repeated four times. This is very close to Matthew 19:14 NIV, which reads, "Jesus said, 'Let the little children come to me, and do not hinder them, for the kingdom of heaven belongs to such as these.'" In this chapter of Matthew, people are attempting to bring their children to Jesus so that he can pray for them, but his disciples stop them. In response, Jesus tells them to let the children come to him.

Another biblical reference surrounding mothers and children occurs in the stunning scene where Offred gives birth alone to her daughter Holly after a brief and painful reunion with her firstborn, Hannah (now Agnes, which means *lamb*). It's a stark scene: A wolf stands on the snow-covered ground, watching Offred silently. Later, when Offred rushes back out into the snow, the wolf eyes her hungrily as she falls to the ground. She ultimately uses a gun to scare the wolf off. This wolf carries biblical significance, specifically in references to lambs among wolves. Luke 10:3 reads

"Go your ways: behold, I send you forth as lambs among wolves," and a similar verse appears in the book of Matthew. Certainly June and both her daughters are like lambs among wolves in Gilead in terms of the ways they are abused and mistreated and how little their lives matter in Gilead beyond their ability to bear children. As we see in the episode, June is also resilient and capable of fighting back and defending herself against the wolves.

The Wedding Ceremony

Season 2, episode 5 ("Seeds"), features wedding ceremonies under the new regime. The preacher who conducts the group marriage, of which Nick and Eden are a part, combines the passage in Genesis that describes the creation of Eve with the curse after the fall in Genesis 3. Nick, when they are all gathered in the sitting room, chooses a kinder passage to recite, and as he does, he looks almost exclusively at Offred: "Love keeps no record of wrongs and endures all things. Love never fails." Here he shortens the famous love passage from Corinthians that Eden will later recite before her execution:

> Love is patient, love is kind. It does not envy, it does not boast, it is not proud. It does not dishonor others, it is not self-seeking, it is not easily angered, it

keeps no record of wrongs. Love does not delight in evil but rejoices with the truth. It always protects, always trusts, always hopes, always perseveres. Love never fails. But where there are prophecies, they will cease; where there are tongues, they will be stilled; where there is knowledge, it will pass away. (1 Corinthians 13:4–8 NIV)

Nick's chosen reading about love contrasts sharply with the manipulative way the wedding ceremony uses Bible verses to condemn and oppress women.

Women and the Bible

Women in Gilead are forbidden from reading, but Offred finds a Bible in Eden's belongings full of Eden's written notes in the margins. After Offred finds Eden's Bible, she shows it to Serena Joy. At first, Serena Joy takes the party line and says, "She was hiding a multitude of sins." But Offred replies, "She was trying to read the Bible! How are you going to keep her [the baby] safe?" Serena Joy tries to stay with the Gilead rhetoric, "She is going to obey God's word." Offred counters, "She won't be able to read it!"

Serena Joy talks the other wives into confronting the ruling body of Gilead to petition them to allow women to read the Bible. Serena Joy walks up to address the Commanders and says, "We propose an amendment." She continues, "The Holy Scripture is a miracle—a gift given by him to all humanity. We believe our sons and daughters should be able to read it." Then she picks up Eden's Bible and reads from the beginning of the Gospel of John, "In the beginning was the Word, and the Word was with God, and the Word was God. He was with God in the beginning. Through him all things were made; without him nothing was made that has been made." Serena Joy chooses a beautiful Scripture to support her stance, the one describing Christ as the metaphorical Word who created the world and all that is in it. In a brutal reminder that Gilead is not interested in the Bible, only in their perverted version of Scripture, the Commanders punish Serena Joy for her reading and her request by cutting off her finger.

Faith and Hope

While religion primarily appears in negative and twisted ways in the series as Gilead appropriates Christianity for its own ends, moments of sincere faith and hope form a powerful contrast. Eden seeks to understand God, and Serena Joy fights for all to be able to read the Bible. June exhibits one of the most explicitly religiously, sincere scenes during the time she spends in the *Boston Globe* office during her escape attempt. In season 2, episode 2 ("Unwomen"), June kneels between two nooses and prays at the memorial wall she has built in the old *Boston Globe* building: "God, by whose mercy the faithful departed have found rest, please send your holy angel to watch over this place. Through Christ our Lord, Amen." She seems to be not only grieving for the ones who died there but also asking for protection for herself. June uses a religious practice to honor and connect with others suffering under Gilead. Even though the Colonies seem to be a hopeless place, similar to June's Wailing Wall, there is also a glimmer of hope when Janine's character meets Emily there. Janine, after being sent to the Colonies, demonstrates a strong faith that she will be delivered. "That's up to God. He holds me in the palm of his hand," she tells Emily, who snidely asks if God couldn't hold her in Bora Bora instead. In season 2, episode 7 ("After"), they see Offred, and Janine proclaims, "God saved us. He has a plan for both of us."

The Hulu series offers more hope than the novel, not only by infusing the story with glimmers of faith but also by extending the resistance storyline, providing hope that things can and will be different someday. The end of season 1 foreshadows season 2's conspiracy of women when June remarks, "They should never have given us uniforms if they didn't want us to be an army." The element of hope strengthens as the women in the story come together to conspire to not "let the bastards win." The community between these women becomes clear and strong in beautiful moments, such as the celebration of names in season 2, episode 7 ("The Other Side"). Offred sees Janine and Emily in the grocery store and on impulse tells them that her name is June. She tells another Handmaid "my name is June." Then the other Handmaids join in: "My name is Brianna." They all start speaking their names, a rising chorus of names, community, and resistance.

One of the main rebels is Emily (the first Ofglen, then Unwoman, then Ofsteven), who fights whenever she gets a chance and seems to finally escape Gilead at the end of season 2. Though it might be hard for people who have only read the book to believe, even Serena Joy is part of this conspiracy of women. Her party-line façade starts to crack in season 2, episode 5 ("Seeds") when she and Offred are on their way to a Prayvaganza and Serena Joy quips about that name: "Not one of the Commander's better efforts if you ask me." In season 2, episode 7 ("After"), Offred and Serena Joy conspire to forge documents from the Commander while he's in the hospital. Significantly, they fake "the counsel of divine law." There's something wonderful and ironic about that detail, that together Serena Joy and Offred dare to rewrite the supposed divine laws that the leaders claimed were inspired by God. The rebellion reaches a pivotal point when the new Ofglen blows up the new Rachel and Leah Center during its dedication ceremony. June continues to be a central figure of resistance, and the end of season 2 sees her saving her daughter Nicole from Gilead and returning to find her first child, Hannah. This sisterhood of rebellion, the insistence of women who know they could be empowered to end Gilead's tyranny, this glimpse toward hope is one of the best parts of season 2. Though religion is used in twisted ways against women and all who resist Gilead's oppressive tyranny, the series provides these contrasting moments of faith and hope that show a better way. We'll see what the powerful forces of faith, hope, and love bring as the story continues in season three.

Acknowledgments

Many, many thanks to Emily Brower, who invited me to write a book I have wanted to write for years and for her invaluable guidance all along the way. I am also grateful to my friend Sarah Dougherty, who edited every chapter and shared her brilliance throughout this process. Thank you to my family for their continued love and support, especially my son Byron, who was particularly interested in this project. I also appreciate the early help from Kyle Archibald and Caleb Crossman. I am grateful for the continued encouragement from my hallway buddies at the university; special thanks to Sam Baker, Allen Jones, Steve Halliday, and Ryan Stark for their advice and general cheerleading. To my students here at Corban, thank you for being a source of continual inspiration and joy. Finally, I'm thankful that, once again, I can wrangle with the need for redemption woven into every story since Eden.

Index